Discovering Education and Society

Discovering Education and Society

A Gandhian Perspective

Edited by
Pankaj Das
Anita Vaidyanathan

SHIPRA

Rs. 995

ISBN: 978-93-88691-87-1

2026 imp., PoD
First Published in 2021

Discovering Education and Society:
A Gandhian Perspective

Published by:
SHIPRA PUBLICATIONS
LG 18-19, Pankaj Central Market
I.P. Ext., Patparganj, Delhi 110092, India
+91 47322068; 96500 28065, 9810522367
info@shiprapublication.com
www.shiprapublication.cpm

Foreword

I know that we live in a society that is not necessarily very positive towards Mohandas Karamchand Gandhi. In fact, it would not be entirely wrong to say that the 'Gandhi-bashing' industry is quite active in our country. Yes, for militant nationalists or the champions of hyper-masculine religious nationalism, Gandhi is an embarrassment, or some sort of 'effeminate' nonsense. For the proponents of identity politics, the 'brahminical' Gandhi has to be continually castigated and separated from the 'subaltern' Ambedkar. Well, the Marxists with their 'science' of historical materialism, it seems, are not very comfortable with the Gandhian 'utopia'; and these days the proponents of the market-driven discourse of neoliberalism are bound to loathe Gandhi's prescription for a non-consumptionist mode of living. Furthermore, as a society, we have almost museumised Gandhi through the process of ritualisation— just pretending to remember him on October 2 and January 30! Otherwise, amid the violence of communalism, militarism and consumerism we kill Gandhi every moment.

Under these circumstances, when I look at a book of this kind, I feel that there are still some scholars, educationists and teachers amongst us who seek to engage with Gandhi with some amount of seriousness. It is in this context that I wish to make three points which, I believe, are absolutely important for rediscovering his educational ideals and politico-spiritual perspectives. First, as we see the crisis of modernity—the way its irresistible urge to dominate and manipulate nature for unlimited techno-economic growth or greed has caused ecological violence and led to a 'risk society'; or the way the prevalent economy or discourse of power has reduced us into robotic performers with docile bodies and minds or restless consumers intoxicated with the glitz of the market, we begin to realize why Gandhi critiqued this 'satanic' civilisation, and pleaded for a kind of 'swaraj' that values harmony, connectedness, decentralisation and simplicity. Yes, his *Hind Swaraj* ought to be read time and again to decolonize our consciousness and rethink modernity. Second, as violence is normalized and even sanctified in the name of 'law and order', 'nationalism' or even 'revolution', the art of living and resistance that Gandhi evolved through the practice of *satyagraha* acquires added relevance. And third, Gandhi was immensely reflexive; he could look at his own follies and mistakes with heightened self-critique; and this enabled him to 'experiment' with truth, religiosity, sexuality and politics. And this immense life-energy of 'experimental' Gandhi manifested itself at Noakhali (now in Bangladesh) in 1946. What an extraordinary effort to restore the language of sanity and cross-religious dialogue in an insane/communally charged world!

Hence, as I feel, Gandhi ought to arouse the interest of those who seek to reimagine education for healing this wounded world (the world filled with authoritarian personalities, suicide bombers, zealots and fundamentalists, and demonic techno-corporate empires), and see beyond what is otherwise regarded as 'mainstream' education: the narcissism of the 'intellect', the acquisition of specialized academic knowledge, or the celebration of egotistic pride for acquiring a university degree. For Gandhi, education ought to be endowed with a radically different meaning. It must 'integrate' us: body and soul, brain and heart, thinking and practice, and study and meaningful labour. Not solely that. Education, he must have felt, ought to arouse the important qualities of living — self-reflection, endurance, art of dialogue, austerity, and the courage to resist evil forces. In a way, he sought to reconcile the secular and the sacred. From the Tolstoy Farm in South Africa to the sites of resistance: Gandhi sought to educate himself perpetually, and through his own life-practice wanted to educate others. In a way, life became a text; the teacher became a student; and togetherness became the spirit of learning.

This edited volume, I have no hesitation in saying, arouses hope in these dark times. The papers—written with great care, qualitative research and intellectual zeal—are bound to invite the readers to the landscape that Gandhi as an amazing politico-spiritual artist sought to portray.

Avijit Pathak
Professor, Centre for the Study of Social Systems,
Jawaharlal Nehru University, New Delhi

Preface

A conflict-ridden world would only perpetuate violence, erosion of value systems, greed, commercialisation and self-centredness where individual aggrandisement comes at the cost of social good. We can raise a self-conscious and mindful generation only through the medium of education, which alone has the power to sensitise, raise awareness, inculcate values and ethics essential for the establishment of a harmonious society. Education alone has the power to develop resilience, which equips the young to learn from adversities and failures and emerge out of a critical situation. The current pandemic is a classic example wherein the entire teaching learning community has transcended the boundations of operating within the confines of their educational spaces through a quick transition to a digital mode of teaching learning. When we talk about resilience, adaptability, problem solving skills and self-reliance as the key tenets of education, it becomes imperative to talk about Mahatma Gandhi's educational ideas and principles which hold relevance in contemporary times.

Mahatma Gandhi was one of the prolific thinkers. His ideas are not only innovative and progressive, but also pragmatic and realistic. His principles of truth, non-violence, fellow feeling resolved many problems in the areas of education, religion, politics, economy, caste, community, nation, etc. Throughout his entire lifespan he experimented with his own ideas and principles. His engagement and involvement with the Tolstoy's Farm to the pivotal role he played in the freedom struggle are classic examples of his experiments.

Gandhi's idea of nation was based on his concept of Buniyadi Shiksha and Nai Taleem. Through his proposal of Buniyadi Shiksha, he wanted to strengthen the indigenous education system in the country. He emphasised on dignity of labour and innovative craft centred education, which aimed to promote vocational education and skill development. He iterated upon certain aspects such as the development of critical thinking, a value-based education system, promotion of Sarvodaya for rural and marginalised sections of society, women empowerment and communal harmony, which could only be achieved through education. For Gandhi, education is not life, it is life. Gandhi in his Buniyadi Shiksha, or Nai Taleem not only advocated free and compulsory education for promoting universalisation of elementary education, but also emphasised upon the principle of human value. Although Buniyadi Shiksha addressed many social and educational problems inherent within the school system, yet it wasn't implemented in the subsequent national educational policies and programmes. In order to address the issues and problems which emerge within the current education system, it is essential for us to revisit and relook at Gandhian principles and ideas.

This edited anthology comprises a plethora of articles which aim to discover the relevance of Gandhian thought and ideals in contemporary times. Professor Avijit Pathak's introduction sets the tone of the book and resonates with our thought process of bringing this anthology at a time when we are battling against the 'crisis of modernity' accompanied with the urge and greed to control and manipulate nature, thereby causing ecological violence and erosion of long-lost values. Gandhian values of harmony and connectedness would enable us to combat the evil forces and reconstruct pedagogic processes to heal the 'wounded world'. The emphasis on holistic education as a pathway for resolving the crisis of the modern world seems to be the way forward. Professor Anil Sadgopal's article, *Nai Taleem: Gandhi's Challenge to Hegemony,* perceives Gandhian model of Nai Taleem as a potent tool to challenge British imperialism, colonial education system, economic, social and gender inequalities. He has critically examined the Macaulayan vis-a-vis the Brahmanical model of education. Education has been perceived as a medium to bring about social transformation. Arushi Kaushik in her article, *Education in Modern Indian Social Thought: Educational Ideas from Gandhi and Tagore's Perspective* explores the similarities and differences in perspective between the two educational thinkers with respect to their ideas on nationalism, modernity and education. Bhumika Rajdev and Anamica Sharma's article, *Revising Gandhi's Idea of Nation and Nationalism: Relevance in Contemporary Education* emphasises on how interweaving the constructs of swarajya, ramrajya and trusteeship into our education system in the conflict-ridden times might lead to the creation of a harmonious and peaceful society. Kamalakanta Roul's article, *Gandhi on Education and Social Transformation: The*

Odishan Way expresses Odishan influence on Gandhian ideologies and principles. Overwhelmed by the sight of extreme poverty in Odisha, Gandhi resorted to scanty mode of dressing — the *lathi, dhoti* and *chadar* and felt inspired to bring about social transformation. The implementation of a model of education based on the principles of non-violence has been delineated by Amila Rupasinghe in her article, *Non-Violence, Education and Harmonious Society: A Strategic Approach to Heal Divided Communities.* Anamika's article, *Gandhi's Philosophy and Human Rights Education,* elaborates on how Gandhi's personal humiliation enabled him to identify with the Indians living in South Africa. The transition of personal hurt into a more expansive nationalistic struggle becomes the foundation of Human Rights Education. The author draws on a broader interpretative framework elaborating on the Gandhian precepts of human dignity and respect as a solid basis for the establishment of Human Rights Education into the curriculum. Ali Haider's article, *Relevance of Gandhian Values in Today's World* emphasises on the need for the integration of Gandhian values such as truth, non-violence, compassion and tolerance into the education curricula. Lata's article, *Sarvodaya: A Gandhian Approach to Upliftment of All* attempts to look at the impact of sarvodaya in relations to the marginalised sections of society. In *Reading Mahatma Gandhi in Today's Text,* Sana Ahmed delineates the role of books, newspaper articles and biographies as powerful educative mediums to orient the youth towards Gandhian values and ideologies. An iconic figure like Gandhi is also subject to scrutiny is vivified through Anita Vaidyanathan's article *Reading Gandhi Through A Feminist Lens: A Gentle Patriarch or A Feminist Humanist.* The article juxtaposes him as a gentle patriarch exerting his charismatic influence over his women associates by involving them in the Bramacharya experiments. Conversely, it also depicts the Mahatma as a feminist humanist through his advocacy of women's rights.

Each article attempts to explore Gandhian precepts, ideologies, values and philosophy through a multidisciplinary framework. Each author has a different take on Gandhi. Thus, the projection of multiple lenses provides the basis of a larger interpretative framework. Gandhi is perceived through the lens of an educationist, philosopher, social scientist and even feminist. While the conglomeration of articles lauds the Mahatma for opposing the colonial system of education and upholding the values *Swarajya, Ramrajya, Ahimsa, Sarvodaya, Truth, Non-Violence and Human Rights,* this book through the analysis of his letters, memoirs and writings enables one to perceive the icon with human failings, without indulging in a deprecatory tone. The book emphasises on the urgent need to restructure education and pedagogy through incorporation of holistic education which aims to integrate the body, mind and soul and paves way for self-reflection, introspection, debate and dialogue. This book will be of relevance to students, Gandhian scholars, policy makers and members of the academia.

This anthology wouldn't have been possible without the unflinching support and contribution of great educators and mentors. We are grateful to Professor Avijit Pathak for having spared his valuable time in writing the Foreword despite his multiple task commitments. We would like to express our gratitude to our teacher and mentor, Professor Anil Sadgopal, for showing his implicit trust in us and sharing his valuable article to be included as a part of this edited anthology. We are also thankful to Shri Rajendra Prasad ji, publisher Sahmat Books, for having given access to Professor Sadgopal's article, which was published in *Social Scientist*, Volume 47, No. 5-6, May-June, 2019. Last but not the least; we are indeed thankful to Shipra Publications for bringing out this anthology.

Pankaj Das
Anita Vaidyanathan

Contents

1

Nai Taleem: Gandhi's Challenge to Hegemony

Anil Sadgopal

Introduction

On 18 March 1922, Gandhiji faced a trial in Ahmedabad on the charge of sedition for writing and publishing 'three seditious and inflammatory articles' in his weekly paper *Young India* during the previous year 1921. "This aroused considerable interest not only in India, but also in Europe, and America.... Never before was such a prisoner arraigned before a British court of justice. Never before were the laws of an all-powerful government so defiantly, yet with such humility, challenged.... Men of all shades of opinion... condemned it in no uncertain term, marvelled at the wisdom, compassion and heroism of the thin spare figure in a loin cloth thundering his anathemas against the Government. And yet none could be gentler nor more sweet-tempered than the prisoner... [who] with a smile and a nod of thanks... for everyone including the prosecutors ... made the occasion momentous and invested the trial with a historic significance.... District and Sessions Judge Robert Broomfield... was mild-mannered and apologetic... gave the impression of a man who was performing a distasteful task with courtesy and good sense... when he took his seat, bowing gravely to the distinguished prisoner. Gandhiji returned the bow.[1]"

---

* The original article was published in *Social Scientist*, Vol. 47, Nos. 5–6, May-June 2019, pp. 9–30. And for this article editors of this book reserved © Anil Sadgopal.

[1] Source: 'The Law and the Lawyers', Gandhi, M. K. (Kher, S. B., Ed.), 1962, 2004, Navjivan Publishing House, Ahmedabad, Gujarat, India, pp. xiii & xvi.

"Gandhiji's speech at the trial pleading guilty to the offence of sedition ... and inviting Judge Broomfield to inflict on him the severest penalty...." even as, in his written statement, he explained "how he had come to lose faith in the British Government and stated that he saw no course open to him but that which he had adopted.[2]" The decisive factor "which made the trial historic was the profound issue involved in it, namely, that of obedience to law as against obedience to moral duty.... The issue raised... was not an isolated, sporadic issue arising from the beach of Section 124A of the Penal Code ... [but] was the perennial issue of Law versus Conscience, an issue of abiding interest to all civilised people of all times... invoked the inalienable moral right and duty to resist a system of governance whose only claim to loyalty and obedience was superior physical might.... [Gandhiji]... sought to establish beyond doubt *the superiority of soul force over sheer force....* a conclusion which will have an abiding purpose and a meaning until humanity survives. [3]"

Challenging Hegemony in Education: The Early Thoughts

The above account of Gandhi's stand in March 1922, while facing the trial on charges of sedition in the British Court, constitutes a powerful evidence of the moral foundation on which he stood gently but firmly. From this foundation, he built his life-long challenge to the hegemonies of all kinds including imperialism, capitalist accumulation of wealth, linguistic domination, inequalities of various kinds, religious fundamentalism, caste oppression and discrimination, gender discrimination, 'English' Education and elite knowledge. Without this sustained reflection, he could not have rebelled against the Macaulayian-cum-*Brahmanical* hegemony over knowledge and education that excludes the majority. This then was the path that eventually led him to develop the concept of *Nai Taleem* (New Education) for social transformation.

There is no known link, ideological or otherwise, between Jotirao Phule and Gandhi, except for a broadly common experience of Indian socio-cultural milieu under the upper caste domination and colonial impact. Yet, Phule's critique of the Macaulayian-cum-*Brahmanical*

---

[2] *Ibid*, p. xviii.

[3] *Ibid*, pp. xix-xx (*Based upon* Chief Justice Shelat's introduction to *The Trial of Gandhi*, Gujarat High Court Publication, 1965, as cited by the Editor Sunit B. Kher).

framework uncannily appears to be a trailblaser[4] of the civilisational debate that Gandhi's Hind Swaraj (1909) initiated a quarter century later questioning the ideology of colonial hegemony and exploitation and its roots in the upper caste control. Gandhi interpreted the British education policy in India in terms of his intuitive understanding, rather than a coherent theory, of the imperialistic design of the British *Raj*. He countered the basic proposition of the colonial rulers with the following assertions:

> "... The foundation that Macaulay laid of education has enslaved us...Is it not a sad commentary that we should have to speak of *Swarajya* [Self-Rule] in a foreign tongue?"
>
> "... by receiving English education, we have enslaved the nation. Hypocrisy, tyranny, etc. have increased; English-knowing Indians have not hesitated to cheat and strike terror into the people."
>
> "... It is we, the English-knowing men, that have enslaved India. The curse of the nation will rest not upon English but upon us."
>
> —*Hind Swaraj* (1909)
> Chapter XVIII

Like Phule, Gandhi, too, was deeply concerned about the outcome of colonial education:

> "Is the goal of the education that you are receiving that of mere employment, whether in the Government departments or other departments? If that be the goal of your education, if that is the goal you have set before yourself, I feel and I fear that the vision which the Poet [Rabindranath Tagore] pictured for himself is far from being realised."
>
> –Cited from an Address to Students, 27 April 1915

Deeply anguished by the Jallianwala Bagh massacre by the British police in 1919, Gandhi gave a nationwide call to the students and teachers in the government (i.e. British government) institutions to quit and set up 'national' institutions dedicated to the cause of constructing

---

[4] Mahatma Jotirao Phule's Memorandum to the Indian Education Commission (i.e. 'Hunter Commission'), 1882.

and imparting 'national' institutions. The years that followed were witness to Gandhi continuously defining and re-defining education as part of the anti-imperialist freedom struggle.

Gandhi raises the level of this debate when he writes:

> "I have never been able to make a fetish of literary training ... literary training by itself adds not an inch to one's moral height and that character building is independent of literary training... the Government schools have unmanned us, rendered us helpless and godless. They have filled us with discontent, and providing no remedy for the discontent, have made us despondent. They have made us what we were intended to become, clerks and interpreters."
>
> –*Young India*, 1 June 1921

> "The curriculum and pedagogic ideas which form the fabric of modern education were imported from Oxford and Cambridge, Edinburgh and London. But they are essentially foreign, and till they are repudiated, there never can be national education... The question then is this: The choice must be clearly and finally made between national and foreign education, the choice of type and archetype, of meaning and purpose, of ends and means." [emphasis mine]
>
> –*Young India*, 20 March 1924

> "... There is no doubt that the young people [children of agriculturists] when they come back knew not a thing about agriculture, were indeed deeply contemptuous of the calling of their fathers ... The fact that the tragedy of this destructive breach was limited by the need of the Government for only a specified number of clerks and deputies, should not really mask the reality of the transaction.... there has never been the remotest perception of the fact that the whole thing is an evil because it was destroying the very foundations of all national life and growth. The system must be scrapped; enquiry must be made promptly as to what constituted the elements of education before Indian Universities [under British *Raj*] were constituted, before Lord Macaulay wrote his fatal Minutes..."
>
> –*Young India*, 20 March 1924

Making a case for what he called 'national education', Gandhi invariably questioned the socio-political character of education imparted in British *Raj*. For instance, in his Convocation Address as the Founding Chancellor of the Gujarat Vidyapeeth, one of the 'national universities' created in response to his call, he contrasts the character of students from Gujarat Vidyapeeth with those of the Government colleges or universities:

> "One of our students has gone to jail in Bardoli [farmers' movement] and many more will go. They are the pride of the Vidyapeeth. Much as they may desire to do likewise, can students of Government institutions dare to do so? It is not open to them to go to Bardoli and help Vallabhbhai [Patel][5], as it is to you. They can only give secret sympathy. What is literary training worth if it cramps and confines us at a critical moment in national life? ..."
>
> –*Young India*, 21 June 1928

Exploring an Alternative Vision

While elaborating the meaning of *swaraj* or self-rule, Gandhi clearly distinguished between the British in India and their 'modern civilisation'. His critique of the exploitative character of 'modern civilisation' enabled him to maintain, "If the English become Indianised, we can accommodate them. If they wish to remain in India along with their [modern] civilisation, there is no room for them" and "... we do not want the tyranny of either English rule or Indian rule[6]." (*Hind Swaraj*, Chapters XIV and XX respectively). Gandhi's struggle for *swaraj* was to be founded on *civilisational, philosophical and moral* awakening of the Indian people. This enlightenment of the masses, therefore, was the purpose of education.

Gandhi's critique of British education in India itself was pregnant with elements of an emerging and evolving vision. Given the insight

[5] The farmer's movement in the Bardoli region of southern Gujarat in 1928 was being led by Sardar Vallabhbhai Patel.

[6] It is worth exploring whether there is any parallel between the Gandhian rejection of 'either English rule or Indian rule' and the unambiguous rejection by Shaheed Bhagat Singh of 'both the white rulers and brown rulers' unless there is socialist reconstruction of Indian society.

gained from his radical educational experiments in South Africa – first at the Phoenix School at the Phoenix Settlement before writing Hind Swaraj (1909) and later at the Tolstoy Farm (1911–13)—combined with his study of the Indian conditions, Gandhi was in a position to offer a constructive alternative to the nation to replace colonial education. Glimpses of his alternative vision, with significant pedagogical implications, can be had in the following statements:

> "I would develop in the child his hands, his brain and his soul. The hands have almost atrophied. The soul has been altogether ignored."
>
> –*Young India*, 12 March 1925

> "When our children are admitted to schools, they need, not slate and pencil and books, but simple village tools which they can handle freely and remuneratively. This means a revolution in educational methods. But nothing short of a revolution can put education within reach of every child of school-going age."
>
> –*Young India*, 11 July 1929

> "... The utterly false idea that intelligence can be developed only through book reading should give place to the truth that the quickest development of the mind can be achieved by the artisan's work being learnt in a scientific manner. True development of the mind commences immediately the apprentice is taught at every step why a particular manipulation of the hand or a tool is required..."
>
> –*Harijan*, 9 January 1937

On the contested question of language and education, Gandhi offers the following straightforward but thought-provoking ideas (*Hind Swaraj*, Chapter XVIII), his critique of 'English Education' notwithstanding:

> "We are so much beset by the disease of civilisation, that we cannot altogether do without English education. Those who have already received it may make good use of it wherever necessary. In our dealings with the English people ... for the purpose of knowing how much disgusted they [the English] have themselves become with their civilisation, we may use or learn English ... Those who have studied English will have to teach *morality to their progeny through their mother tongue,** and to teach them another Indian

language; but when they have grown up, they may learn English, the ultimate aim being that we should not need it.... A little thought should show you that immediately *we cease to care for English degrees, the rulers will prick up their ears.*" [emphasis mine]

[*Note on 'Those who have studied English ... *through their mother-tongue*': "Gandhi makes a noteworthy distinction here between using English for the acquisition of *secular* knowledge and using the mother-tongue for the acquisition of *ethical* knowledge." - Cited from Parel, 1997, p. 104, Footnote 207.]

"... I think that we have to improve all our languages.... Those English books which are valuable we should translate into the various Indian languages.... And, if we can do this, we can drive the English language out of the field in a short time. All this is necessary for us slaves. Through our slavery the nation has been enslaved, and it will be free with our freedom."

What is *Nai Taleem*?

Gandhi's early experience of the Phoenix School and the Tolstoy Farm in South Africa during the first decade of the twentieth century followed by that of the 'national' universities (*Vidyapeeths*) during 1920s laid the foundations from which Gandhi developed his empirical and intuitive insight into the concept of *Nai Taleem*. The ideas of *Nai Taleem* were successively articulated by Gandhi in *Harijan* during 1930's. Several of the concerns raised by intellectuals who disagreed with the evolving Gandhian conception, partly or wholly, were also reported in *Harijan* to which Gandhi would respond explaining and, when it became necessary, even modifying his stand. This was also the period when the intellectual exchange on several profound philosophical and political issues between Gandhi and Tagore peaked, though it had started in 1914–15 when Gandhi along with the students of his Phoenix School visited Tagore's Satiniketan (Bhattacharya, 1997). Far more significantly, this was also the period when the historic Gandhi-Ambedkar debate on the question of *Brahmanical* hegemony, the implications of the caste system and the role of social justice drew nation-wide attention - starting from the debate in the Yerwada prison in Pune, leading to the Poona Pact (1932) and later in the wake of the publication of Dr. Ambedkar's seminal essay, *Annihilation of Caste* (1936). There is no better way to comprehend *Nai Taleem* than to analyse the progression of educational ideas during the three decades between the writing of *Hind Swaraj* and Gandhi's formal address at the Wardha educational conference in 1937. This should, I have no doubt, constitute one of the most inspiring chapters in the world history of education.

The Wardha Conference (1937)

It was in the backdrop of the above rapidly evolving critical discourse on the impact of *Brahmanical* hegemony and colonialism on Indian society that an 'All India Educational Conference' was organised at Wardha (then in the Central Provinces, now in Maharashtra) in October 1937 under Gandhi's leadership. Since Gandhi had planned to talk on how to transform the entire education system of independent India, he had specially invited the teachers of the 'National Schools' and the 'National Universities' as well as the Education Ministers of seven states where Indian National Congress had formed the newly elected provincial governments. In his address to the Conference, Gandhi unfolded his revolutionary plan to liberate India from Macaulayian-cum-*Brahmanical* education and establish in its place what he called Basic Education Scheme (*Buniyadi Shiksha*), later incorporated in the broader canvas of *Nai Taleem*. It would be worthwhile to cite from this address what gives us a glimpse into the social and pedagogic essence of his vision:

> "What I am going to place before you today is *not about a vocation* that is going to be imparted alongside education. Now, I wish to say that whatever is taught to children, *all of it should be taught necessarily through the medium of a trade or a handicraft* ... We aim at *developing the intellect also with the aid of a trade or a handicraft* ... instead of merely teaching a trade or a handicraft, we may as well educate the children entirely through them. Look at *takli* [spindle] itself, for instance. The lesson of this *takli* will be the first lesson of our students through which they would be able *to learn a substantial part of the history of cotton, Lancashire and the British empire...* How does this *takli* work? What is its utility? And what are the strengths that lie within it? Thus the child learns all this in the midst of play. Through this he also acquires some knowledge of mathematics. When he is asked to count the number of cotton threads on *takli* and he is asked to report how many did he spin, it becomes possible to acquaint him step by step with good deal of mathematical knowledge through this process. And the beauty is that none of this becomes even a slight burden on his mind. The learner does not even become aware that he is learning. While

> playing around and singing, he keeps on turning his *takli* and from this itself he learns a great deal." [emphasis mine]
>
> –Excerpted from the address by Mahatma Gandhi at the Wardha Education Conference, 22 October 1937 *[Translated from Hindustani by the author; Source: Hindustani Talimi Sangh, 1957, pp. vii-viii]*

Gandhi further elaborates upon his *Nai Taleem* pedagogy:

> "Our education has got to be revolutionised. The *brain must be educated through the hand.* If I were a poet, I could write poetry on the possibilities of the five fingers. Why should you think that the mind is everything and the hands and feet nothing? Those who do not train their hands, who go through the ordinary rut of education, lack 'music' in their life. All their faculties are not trained. Mere book knowledge does not interest the child so as to hold his attention fully. The brain gets weary of mere words, and the child's mind begins to wander. The hand does the things it ought not to do, the eye sees the things it ought not to see, the ear hears the things it ought not to hear, and they do not do, see or hear, respectively what they ought to. They are not taught to make the right choice and so their education often proves their ruin. An *education which does not teach us to discriminate between good and bad, to assimilate the one and eschew the other* is a misnomer." [emphasis mine]
>
> –Discussion with Teacher Trainees, *Harijan*, 18 February 1939[7]

The Spear-head of a Silent Social Revolution

An urgent clarification is necessary at this juncture. *Nai Taleem*, as conceived by Gandhi, covers a much larger and multi-dimensional canvas than just a change in the method of teaching or learning in the schools, colleges or universities. As noted in Section 2.0, the Gandhian pedagogy cannot be viewed in isolation of the *civilisational, philosophical and moral* context of the struggle for *swaraj* in which it took shape.

It is in this historical and contextual conception of pedagogy that we must examine the significance of the Gandhian pedagogy. Only then we will understand why *Nai Taleem* cannot be just adjusted in the prevailing curriculum but calls for a paradigm shift in the entire

[7] *The Collected Works of Mahatma Gandhi (CW)*, Vol. 68, pp. 372–73.

education system and its Macaulayian-cum-*Brahmanical* policy framework. The original Gandhian proposal of Basic Education (*Buniyadi Shiksha*) presented at the Wardha Conference as an educational programme attempted to *place productive manual work at the centre of the school curriculum* from which would emerge *knowledge, values and skills* in an organic manner. This pedagogy, as we will see later, has unprecedented transformative potential at economic and socio-cultural level, especially in the context of the caste-based social hierarchal discriminatory structures (see Section 4.0).

Concerned about the villages becoming "a mere appendage to the cities" and being exploited by the latter, Gandhi envisages the following transformative role for *Nai Taleem*:

> "[*Nai Taleem*] will provide a healthy and moral basis of relationship between the city and the village and thus go a long way towards eradicating ... poisoned relationship between the classes. It will check the progressive decay of our villages and lay the foundation of a juster social order in which there is no unnatural division between the 'haves' and the 'have-nots' and everybody is assured of a living wage and the right to freedom. And all this would be accomplished without the horror of a bloody class war or a colossal capital expenditure such as would be involved in the mechanisation of a vast continent like India... Lastly, by obviating the necessity for highly specialised talent, it would place the destiny of the masses, as it were, in their own hands."
>
> –*Harijan*, 9 October 1937

Gandhi himself elaborates upon his conception of Basic Education "as the spear-head of a silent social revolution fraught with the most far-reaching consequences" (*Harijan*, 9 October 1937). While seeking to reconstruct the curriculum of schools, colleges and universities as per Gandhi's vision, we need to be conscious of the ethical, political and social dimensions, apart from the civilisational and philosophical dimensions, *of pedagogic integration of work with the learning process.*

The Defining Elements

The central thesis as it emerged from the Wardha Conference address (1937), along with the elaborations and clarifications offered by Gandhi elsewhere in his writings, permits us to present the four defining elements of *Nai Taleem*.

A. Holistic Approach: Integration of Head, Heart and Hand[8]

In Gandhi's conception, child development is holistic i.e. constitutive of integration of head, heart and hand. He advances his principal thesis: "Man is neither mere intellect, nor the gross animal body, nor the heart or soul alone... A proper and harmonious combination of all the three is required for the making of the whole man and constitutes the true economics of education." (*Harijan*, May 1937). A researcher summarises Gandhi's concern as follows:

> "... widespread neglect of this principle is everywhere evident, not only amongst the unlettered but also amongst the so-called educated. He [Gandhi] finds in the villages that the endless mechanical drudgery of the labourers deprives them of all scope for developing their mind and soul ... Equally in the schools and colleges of the cities, he finds that intellectual training, divorced as it is from physical work, produces an imbalance just as pernicious. And as for the 'faculties of the heart' of such students, they are simply allowed to 'run to seed or to grow anyhow in a wild and undisciplined manner.' 'The result' he [Gandhi] laments, 'is moral and spiritual anarchy' (Fagg, 2002, p. 9)."

Gandhi had himself often admitted that he had hardly any knowledge of educational theory. He was primarily guided by his common sense, experience and intuition. Yet, his central thesis on viewing productive work as a pedagogic medium is widely acknowledged as a sound pedagogy for harmonious development of 'head, heart and hand' or 'body, mind and spirit' even today[9].

B. Productive Manual Labour as Pedagogic Medium

The proposal to place *productive manual labour at the centre of the curriculum*, to view it as a moral and transformative force and to use it as a pedagogic medium was truly a revolutionary concept. This was so not only in the late 1930s when Gandhi conceived it but continues to challenge the imagination of the educationists around the world

---

[8] Adapted from Fagg (2002), pp. 8–9.

[9] Gandhi's conception of harmonious development of 'head, heart and hand' or 'body, mind and soul' is akin to the contemporary view of the taxonomy of education in terms of three major domains of learning viz. cognitive, affective and psycho-motor skills.

seven decades later too. It provided a materialist and scientific basis for constructing knowledge, evolving values and building multiple skills. Its civilisational, philosophical and ethical implications for reconstructing the very idea of education in the context of social change could not be just wished away. The pedagogic potential of productive work was articulated by Gandhi so powerfully that it made the Indian educational establishment of the British *Raj* as well as the elite sections of the Indian society, embedded as they were in Colonial-cum-*Brahminical*[10] paradigm, visibly uncomfortable. Gandhi faced sharp criticism and protest, amounting to even ridicule. In Gandhi's own words, "This is a libel on me." (*Hairijan*, 18 February 1939). Attempts were made to reduce Gandhian Basic Education to mere vocational education or to restrict its scope to rural population or the poor strata. The most potent cynical attack was in terms of divesting the entire proposal of its transformative potential by de-linking it from its civilisational, philosophic and moral foundations.

C. Mother Tongue

We have already noted earlier how Gandhi responded to the Macaulayian policy of denigrating Indian languages as viable media of providing education and using English to co-opt the upper classes in India as an ally who "may be interpreters between us [i.e. British] and the millions whom we govern." The use of mother tongue in education and the development of Indian languages was one issue on which there was a fairly broad consensus in the nationalist movement (Naik, 1979, p. 4). Enriching the prevailing discourse, Gandhi contended that "We have

---

[10] The term '*Brahmanical*' is used in this paper strictly to refer to the historically embedded ideology of socio-cultural hegemony in India which has been systematically challenged by various social reform movements of 19th and 20th centuries, led by Phule, Narayan Guru, Periyar, Ambedkar and Gandhi. The national freedom movement incorporated the notions of modernity that would further attrition the stranglehold of this ideology. This struggle greatly influenced the manner in which the principles of equality and social justice were enshrined in the Constitution, primarily under Dr. Ambedkar's visionary leadership. The term '*Brahmanical*', therefore, should in no way be seen as a reference to individual members of either the *Brahman* or other upper caste communities. On the contrary, one expects such upper caste/class citizens to join the historically exploited castes and other sections of societies in their continuing struggle against the ideology of *Brahmanism* in fulfillment of the goals of Indian Constitution. Indeed, the *Brahmanical* ideology is so hegemonic that even the leadership of the historically exploited castes has to be on the guard to consciously resist its onslaught on their mind.

to make them [i.e. Indian languages] true representatives of our culture, our civilisation, of the true genius of our nation. (*Harijan*, 5:324)" He warned that education through English medium has resulted in "a permanent bar between the highly educated few and the uneducated many" (*Harijan*, 5:282) and "made our children practically foreigners in their own land" (*Young India*, 1 September 1921). Addressing the students at the Banaras Hindu University, Gandhi provoked them:

> "I am hoping that this University will see to it that the youths who come to it will receive their instruction through the medium of their vernaculars. Our language is the reflection of ourselves, and if you tell me that our languages are too poor to express the best thought, then I say that the sooner we are wiped out of existence the better for us. Is there a man who dreams that English can ever become the national language of India? (Cries of 'Never') Why this handicap on the nation? ... every Indian youth, because he reached his knowledge through the English language, *lost at least six precious years of life...*" [emphasis mine]
>
> –Gandhi's Speech at Banaras Hindu University, 6 February 1916 (*Collected Works* 13, pp. 211–12)

In Gandhi's perception, "the foreign medium has caused brain fag, put an undue strain upon the nerves of our children, made them crammers and imitators, unfitted them for original work and thought, and disabled them for filtrating their learning to the family or the masses ... prevented the growth of our vernaculars..." (*Young India*, 1 September 1921). In *Nai Taleem*, therefore, there would be no option other than having the mother tongue as the primary medium of education from "KG to PG", with the state language, with or without Hindi or English, being taught as separate subjects as per the needs of the region.

D. The Principle of Self-Support

What probably became the most controversial element in *Nai Taleem* was the principle of self-supporting education[11] advanced by Gandhi as being inalienable from his educational vision. Whether intended by Gandhi or not, the principle of self-supporting education became

[11] This is not to be confused at all with the neo-liberal conception of 'self-financing courses' being promoted in the higher education system in India as a public policy for the past two decades.

intertwined with the issue of prohibition or foregoing liquor revenue that was engaging the newly elected Congress Ministries in provinces. In Gandhi's words:

> "The cruelest irony of the new Reforms lies in the fact that we are left with nothing but the liquor revenue to fall back upon in order to give our children education. That is the *educational puzzle* but it should not baffle us... It must be shameful and humiliating to think that unless we got the drink revenue, our children would be starved of their education." [emphasis mine]
>
> –*Harijan*, 21 August 1937 (*Collected Works* 66, p. 57)

It was probably this dilemma that led Gandhi to infer that "we cannot hope to fulfill our obligations to the nation ... if the programme is to depend on money." He, therefore, resolved the issue by advocating a national system of education that would be self-supporting:

> "I have therefore made bold, even at the risk of losing all reputation for constructive ability, to suggest that education should be self-supporting ... I would therefore begin the child's education by teaching it a useful handicraft and enabling it to produce from the moment it begins its training. Thus every school can be made self-supporting, *the condition being that the State takes over the manufactures of these schools.*"
>
> –*Harijan*, 31 July 1937 (*Collected Works* 65, p. 450)

Some of the contemporary intellectuals suspected the motive of the Gandhian proposal of using handicraft as a means of education precisely because it appeared to be a strategy to solve the financial question faced by the provincial Congress Ministries who were under pressure to fulfill their promise of total prohibition, rather than a preferred pedagogy for purposeful education. Others contended, and rightly so, that it is the State's obligation to finance education and, in no case, the children should be asked to earn money to pay for teachers' salaries. Still others attacked the idea by claiming that this would amount to legitimizing child labour. Gandhi, however, was undeterred. In September 1937, he warned against the assumption that the idea of self-supporting education sprang from the necessity of achieving total prohibition at the earliest. "Both are independent necessities," he said as he responded to an educationist's queries. Gandhi continued, "Let us now ... concentrate on educating the child properly through manual work, *not as a side activity, but as the prime means of intellectual training.*" [emphasis mine] While agreeing with the pedagogic content of the proposal, the educationist was not convinced as to why this should be linked to supporting of school's finances. Gandhi responded:

> "*This will be the test of its value.* The child at the age of 14, that is, after finishing seven years' course, should be discharged as an earning unit... You impart education and simultaneously cut at the root of unemployment." [emphasis mine]
>
> –*Harijan*, 18 September 1937 (*Collected Works* 66, pp. 137–39)

There are two ways of looking at the above response. First, Gandhi was primarily advocating a programme of vocational education that would promote rural employment through skill training in traditional occupations. Second, the above was indeed a part of his pedagogy for holistic education for integrating the education of 'head, heart and hand' or 'body, mind and soul'. Here are some helpful clues that tilt the balance in favour of the latter interpretation of Gandhi's mind. While continuing the above dialogue with the educationist, Gandhi said:

> "You have to train the boys in one occupation or another. Round this special occupation you will *train up his mind, his body, his writing, his artistic sense, and so on.*" [emphasis mine] (*ibid.*)

Let us also return to the Wardha Conference held a month after the above dialogue between Gandhi and his questioning educationist. In his address to the Conference, Gandhi was unambiguous when he emphasised that "What I am going to place before you today is *not about a vocation* that is going to be imparted alongside education." His entire elaboration of using *takli* (spindle) that followed was about how this simple spinning device can act as a powerful pedagogic medium for learning mathematics, physics and history without becoming a burden on the child. There is yet another argument that needs to be offered in favour of the primary motivation of the Gandhian proposal being pedagogic, self-supporting or not. While defending his idea of self-supporting education, Gandhi asserted "That would be the test of its [i.e. productive manual work's] value". Indeed, this statement has far-reaching pedagogic implications, irrespective of whether it is seen in its economic or educational dimension, or both. Why should we restrict its meaning to merely the product's economic or marketable value? Without applying "the test of its value", the pedagogic power of productive work would steadily wither away and the latter would fail to be an effective medium of knowledge, values and multiple skills. Any engagement in the productive process implies *pre-planned, disciplined, assiduous and scientific work with tools and materials* until the intended product of social utility is ready. Any lack of rigour in this pedagogic practice is bound to lead to failure in "the test of its [i.e. productive manual work's] value", while also failing in the market!

Now we will dwell upon why Gandhi insisted on the self-supporting element of his proposal, apart from its pedagogic significance, even at the "risk of losing all reputation for constructive ability". An observation by Gandhi during the Wardha Address gives us an insight into his mind. While advocating that the value of the product from the handicraft should be adequate for meeting the cost of the teacher, he said:

> "It is neither possible for us to keep waiting until the [British] government gives us adequate funds out of its treasury *nor until the Viceroy reduces the military expenditure* or some other similar way out is found." [emphasis mine]
>
> –Excerpted from the address by Mahatma Gandhi at the Wardha Education Conference, 22 October 1937
> *[Translated from Hindustani by the author; Source: Hindustani Talimi Sangh, 1957, p. x]*

Clearly, Gandhi's insistence on self-supporting principle in education cannot be delinked from its historical context of the colonial rule when the foreign government was not even expected to change its economic priorities in favour of the people's interest. Gandhi had the experience of leading several political negotiations with the representatives of the British *Raj* during 1920s and 1930s. He must have, therefore, known without an iota of doubt that mass education and, that too, of social relevance, would be least of the priorities for the colonial administration in India. It sounds reasonable for him, therefore, to speak of self-supporting education during the colonial rule, so that education can be spread among the masses. Also, it would be naïve to expect the colonial administration to finance the radical anti-colonial ideas of Gandhian education, unless the British *Raj* was ready to commit suicide! The question, therefore, is reformulated:

Would Gandhi have given up his insistence on making education self-supportive if this question is considered in the context of the State in independent India? The answer is probably both 'Yes' and 'No'.

In an article on higher education published in *Harijan* (9 July 1938), Gandhi sums up his position in a five-point statement. Two out of these dealing with the issue of financing education are cited below:

- "The State must pay for it wherever it has *definite use* for it."
- "I am opposed to *all* higher education being paid from the general revenue." [emphasis mine]

Elsewhere in the same article, there was also a reference to the desirability of the universities being self-supporting. An ex-professor wrote to Gandhi seeking clarification, especially in the context of the second of the above statements. Gandhi published a detailed response, some extracts of which are reproduced below:

> "My article is clear enough if the expression *'definite use'* mentioned in it is given its extensive meaning... I have pictured to myself an India [presumably post-independence India] continually progressing along the lines best suited to her genius... everyone of the seven lakhs of villages becomes a well-living republic in which there are no illiterates, in which no one is idle for want of work, in which everyone is usefully occupied and has nourishing food, well-ventilated dwellings, and sufficient *Khadi* for covering the body, and in which all the villagers know and observe the laws of hygiene and sanitation, *such a State must have varied and increasing needs, which it must supply* unless it would stagnate. I can therefore well imagine the State financing all the education my correspondent mentions and much more that I could add... What, however, ... *the State will not have is an army of B.A.'s and M.A.'s* with their brains sapped with too much cramming and minds almost paralysed by the impossible attempt to speak and write English like Englishmen. The majority of these will have no work, no employment... *most of the knowledge gained during their twelve years of High Schools and Colleges is of no use whatsoever to them.*" [emphasis mine]
>
> "*University training becomes self-supporting when it is utilised by the State.* It is criminal to pay for a training which benefits neither the nation nor the individual... [since] the existing Higher Education,

and for that matter both Primary and Secondary, are not connected with realities, it cannot be of benefit to the State. When it is directly based on realities and is wholly given through the mother tongue ... *To be based on realities is to be based on national, i.e.; State, requirements. And the State will pay for it...*" [emphasis mine]

–*Harijan*, 30 July 1938 (*Collected Works* 67, pp. 210–12)

Social Character of Productive Work and Knowledge: Anti-Caste Implications

In this section, we would dwell upon how the Gandhian pedagogy provides us with an essential basis for resisting discrimination, rooted in caste, patriarchy and other *Manuwadi* structures - historically practiced in Indian society and institutionalised in the education system. The exclusionary character of the education system has been further reinforced by the globalised economic order during the past three decades. Policy analysis undertaken in recent years reveals how the neo-liberal policies have introduced trade and profit in education as new instruments of distortion of knowledge, exclusion through privatisation and commercialisation and increased discrimination through the multi-layered schools and colleges (Sadgopal, 2010a). It must be recognised that the Gandhian pedagogy demands fundamental structural and conceptual changes in the education system, almost amounting to a paradigm shift.

To place the following discussion in perspective, it is pertinent to refer to the 1936 debate between Dr. Ambedkar and Gandhi when the arguments and counter-arguments of both over 'Annihilation of Caste' were serialised in Gandhi's *Harijan*. Clearly, to the readers today, the debate over '*Varna* vs. Caste' was decisively won by Dr. Ambedkar on the basis of his scholarly and logical articulation of history and sociology. However, few realise that this debate had a lasting impact on Gandhi's mind. His address at the Wardha Conference (1937) bears evidence. By placing productive work at the centre of the curriculum of post-independence India's classrooms, the socio-political equation between the *dalits*, tribals, OBCs and the Muslims (today's Bahujans), on the one hand, and the upper classes/castes, on the other, is bound to undergo a significant transformation. The oppressed sections, denied education so far, would become the leaders in the acquisition of knowledge when the children would learn in productive teams, rather than from the prescribed textbooks.

The Non-Gandhian Sources

Nai Taleem constitutes a radical departure from this *Brahmanical*-cum-colonial paradigm in so far it challenges the dichotomy by placing productive manual work at the centre of school curriculum itself[12]. To be sure, Gandhi was neither the only one nor the first one to conceive of this idea. Similar notions of work-centred curriculum have been practiced in varying manners in different countries of the west, including the erstwhile USSR and other socialist countries. Parel (1997) records that "Gandhi came to appreciate it from his readings of Ruskin, Tolstoy and Bondaref", though "Manual labour, extolled here [i.e. in *Hind Swaraj*], is not a valued activity according to the norms of traditional [Hindu] civilisation" that Gandhi relied upon (*ibid*, p. 69, Footnote 130). Thirty years before Gandhi's address at the Wardha Conference, the famous American philosopher, psychologist and educational reformer John Dewey (1907) advanced a coherent social theory calling for introducing occupations into school for educational purposes and argued strongly in favour of introducing work-centred education in all American schools.

Delinking Productive Work from its Roots of Discrimination and Injustice

Let us begin with Gandhi's choice of occupations as productive tasks to be brought at the centre of curriculum. A list can be made on the basis of the accounts available from various Basic Education (*Buniyadi Shiksha*) institutions that sprung up in various parts of the country in the wake of Wardha Conference. The list (not exhaustive) of occupations is given in Table 1.

What is striking about the list is the social character of the occupations. Without exception, all the listed occupations involve manual work and are undertaken primarily by the historically oppressed classes/castes viz. *Dalits*, tribals, OBCs and Muslim artisans

[12] We take due note of the debate regarding the 'casteist' interpretations of the Gandhian proposal of introducing productive tasks related to the SCs, STs, most OBCs, Muslim artisans and other lower caste communities (the *Bahujans*) in the curriculum. Given the discriminatory practices institutionalised in Indian social structures, there is indeed adequate and justified ground for such fears if the Gandhian pedagogy is pursued. At the same time, we note the radical implications of this agenda which was at the root of the Gandhian programme of social transformation through *Nai Taleem*. This is precisely why the Gandhian proposal met with such fierce and irrational resistance from the upper caste/class and other elite sections of society (Richards, 2001; Fagg, 2002; Krishna Kumar, 2005; NCERT, 2007).

Table 1: Occupations Selected for the Gandhian Programme of Basic Education
(Period: From 1938 onwards)

Spinning	Leather Curing (Tanning)
Weaving	Shoe Making
Dyeing cloth	Tailoring
Farming	Ironsmithy & Metal Work
Animal Husbandry & Dairying	Carpentry
Manual Agro-processing	Tool Making
Forestry	Printing
Horticulture	Construction
Building & Cleaning Latrines	Alternative Energy (e.g. Gobar Gas Plant)
Pottery	Gathering and Using Minor Forest Produce

(the Bahujans), with the women in each of these social categories playing a significant role. Occupations like leather curing (tanning) and shoemaking are performed by *Chamars* (Madigas in Andhra Pradesh, Arundhatiyars in Tamil Nadu), who are placed at the lowest social order even among the *Dalits*. In the Indian socio-economic structure, these hereditary occupations, for centuries, have stood entirely marginalised and carried the stigma of being inferior to the occupations of the upper classes/castes. In addition, these occupations are also at the bottom of the Indian wage structure and the surplus extracted therefrom has been used for creating wealth for few both during the feudal period and the modern period of capitalist growth.

The Gandhian programme of Basic Education for post-independence India proposed *to place these occupations of the lowest social order at the centre of school curriculum* and pedagogically link them with knowledge, values and skills. The political message is inescapable: *Accord these occupations and the communities engaged in them a place of dignity that was never their destiny in Indian history.* Gandhi had invariably recognised that all such productive tasks had a strong knowledge-cum-skill content, including scientific, along with their context of socio-cultural history. A recent study has further provided documentary evidence in support of the scientific and technical content of the productive tasks undertaken historically by a range of the oppressed castes in various parts of India (Ilaiah, 2007). Further substantiating Gandhi's thesis, this study reveals the rich pedagogical base for learning, value formation and building skills available in productive work undertaken by the oppressed castes.

It may not be overemphasised that this radical feature of the Gandhian proposal could not have been drawn at all from the *Brahmanical* roots in ancient Indian traditions. In this context, it would be worthwhile to cite the following perceptive commentary by Krishna Kumar (2005),

> "... [Gandhian pedagogy] implied a violation of India's old concepts of learning. The epistemology of 'basic education' was thoroughly radical, and there is no way we can place it in the context of ancient Indian traditions ... it implied a radical restructuring of school knowledge. Productive handicrafts had been associated in Indian society with the lowest placed groups in the hierarchy of castes... [pre-colonial] education ... favoured the skills and knowledge systems on which the upper castes had monopoly... literacy, literary knowledge and accounting procedures were the staple of pre-colonial education. Both the skills and the content associated with these basic features of the curriculum of indigenous education represented the material and cultural interests of the upper castes."
>
> "... 'Basic education' involved direct conflict with the indigenous tradition because it introduced into the school curriculum a form of knowledge on which low caste groups had monopoly. This kind of knowledge ... was announced to be the core curriculum. In a school following this curriculum, a low-caste child would feel far more at home than an upper-caste child. Both in terms of worldview and functional skills, the curriculum of a 'basic school' favoured the child belonging to the lowest stratum of society. From this point of view, Gandhi's proposal intended to make the education system stand on its head..."
>
> –Kumar, Krishna (2005)
> In *Political Agenda of Education*, pp. 179–80

However, Krishna Kumar's hope that "the curriculum of a 'basic school' favoured the child belonging to the lowest stratum of society" will hold true only if the Gandhian programme is implemented in a fully public-funded Common School System based in Neighbourhood Schools aimed at guaranteeing education of equitable quality for all children, irrespective of their economic, socio-cultural, locational, linguistic or gender backgrounds or disability, physical or mental. If this crucial enabling condition along with other essential features of the curriculum, as spelt out in the following Sections, are not ensured and we continue with the present multi-layered school system rooted in discrimination, the Gandhian Basic Education would remain a non-starter, just as it has since the Wardha Conference in 1937.

No wonder, the Indian state has steadfastly rejected the Gandhian proposal since independence, including the latest attempt in 2004–05, as briefly recorded below.

Enabling Conditions for Gandhi's Work-Centred Education

In 2004–05, the NCERT was asked by the then UPA-1 Central Government to undertake a thorough review of the National Curriculum Framework–2000 (NCF-2000) and prepare a new National Curriculum Framework–2005 (NCF-2005) for the whole country. As a part of this exercise, NCERT constituted 21 National Focus Groups (NFGs) to write 'Position Papers' on various aspects of education. One of them was constituted on 'Work and Education', presumably to take a fresh look at the Gandhian *Nai Taleem* and suggest ways and means to incorporate at least its pedagogic essence in NCF-2005[13]. The NFG Position Paper on 'Work and Education' listed certain "enabling conditions" without which the work-centred education cannot be institutionalised in the national system of education. These are summarised below (NCERT, 2007, pp. 54–55):

- A Common School System [based on Neighbourhood Schools] with certain *non-negotiable minimum* infrastructural, curricular and pedagogic norms that will include all schools, irrespective of the type of their management, sources of income or the affiliating Boards of Examinations; work-centred education would be *a non-starter as long as it is not implemented in all the schools within a declared timeframe.*
- All schools initially up to elementary stage (Class VIII) to act as genuine Neighbourhood Schools in both rural and urban

[13] The National Focus Group (NFG) on 'Work and Education' was constituted under my chairpersonship and its elaborate report was uploaded on NCERT's website in 2005–06 and published in 2007. None of its key ideas could be incorporated into NCF-2005, despite Late Prof. Yash Pal being Chairperson of the NCF National Steering Committee and Prof. Krishna Kumar, the then Director, NCERT, being one of its most knowledgeable members. Further, it did not make any difference either that I was also a member of the same Committee. All my pleadings and hard-headed negotiations came to a naught. Gandhi's appeal for making *Nai Taleem* the basic framework of education in post-Independence India could have not asked for more fortuitous circumstances than what we had in 2004–05.

areas; this is to be extended up to [senior secondary] stage in a phased manner within a declared timeframe.

- The National Curriculum Framework and core curriculum as approved in the national policy to be applicable to all schools including the private unaided schools; within these broad parameters, each school or a school cluster to have full flexibility for negotiating its own curriculum and adopting contextual texts and teaching-learning processes.
- A system of process-based assessment (both formative and summative) based upon such evaluation parameters as will test the attributes that are expected to develop amongst children from work-centred education; public examination system as well as competitive entrance tests to be restructured in order to incorporate these principles of assessment.... And
- Legislation to ensure *education of equitable quality* for all children.

The Position Paper finally suggested a detailed five-year roadmap of phase-wise planned transition which in turn is based upon the lessons drawn from the historical overview and critique of policy and practice undertaken in the NFG Position Paper. These lessons are enumerated below (*ibid.*, pp. 56–58):

First, the time for experiments is long over as a wealth of knowledge and experience in relating work with education is already available, both within and outside the country.

Second, directionless, dithering and ambiguous steps for endlessly 'incremental' implementation in bits and pieces and, that too, without appropriate policy changes, timeframe or adequate resource allocation at the national level, will just not work. What is instead called for, to begin with, is an unambiguous declaration of *all* the necessary policy changes with a clear timeframe for phase wise and nation-wide implementation of both work-centred education *in the entire school system* (including the private unaided schools) and Vocational Education and Training Programme (VET) *outside* the school system.

Third, it is a widespread *misconception that curricular reforms can be de-linked from structural changes* in the school system.

Fourth, it is wrong to assume that implementation of curricular reform in a category of schools (e.g. government/local body schools) can be sustainable, while keeping the rest of the schools unreformed. The *process of curricular reform has to cover the entire school system, including the private unaided schools, in order to become sustainable.* It is nobody's case, however, that the full coverage can happen overnight by a *diktat* from above but there has to be a credible policy-level declaration of a *phase-wise plan to make the full switchover within a specified timeframe* so that the general public has the confidence that their children are not being treated as guinea pigs.

Let us recall that "no developed or developing country has ever achieved Universalisation of Elementary Education (UEE) without a powerful state-funded Common School System with Neighbourhood Schools. India is not going to be an exception either to this historical experience. *And without an effective and universal programme of work-centred education, it is unlikely that UEE (and later Universal Secondary Education too) would succeed!*" (*ibid.*, p. 58)

The proposed radical departure from the present educational system would not be obviously possible without building up *a nation-wide social movement* in its support. In this sense, the present paper is to be viewed as an advocacy document for various sections of society, including the policy makers and political parties.

None of the key philosophical, curricular and/or pedagogic ideas or the elements of the action plan could be incorporated in the NCF-2005 (see Footnote 13). It is tempting to recall Gandhi's harsh words (see Section 1.0), "The system must be scrapped; enquiry must be made promptly as to what constituted the elements of education before Indian Universities [under British *Raj*] were constituted, before Lord Macaulay wrote his fatal Minutes... (*Young India*, 20 March 1924)."

Epilogue

At the end of the Wardha Conference on education in October 1937, Gandhi said, "I have given many things to India. But this system of education ...is, I feel, the best of them. I do not think I will have anything better to offer to the country." Yet, what to Gandhi was his best gift to India is precisely what the Indian State has refused to accept to date. This must be acknowledged as one of the greatest ironies of India's struggle for *swaraj*. Our freedom struggle is possibly unique in the world history of anti-colonial struggles in the sense that it encompassed building a nationalist alternative vision of education. Yet, India continues to adhere to the Macaulayian-cum-*Brahmanical* framework, in its tragically worsening metamorphosis!

The Gandhian vision of education was obliterated as a result of the battle between the two mutually exclusive models of development viz., industrialised, centralised and urban-oriented capitalist model *versus* village-based, decentralised and basically socialistic model calling for resource redistribution. To be sure, the dominant capitalist development model, despite its strong foundation in the Public Sector, was premised on the argument that the problems of poverty, disparity and exploitation will be taken care of by the 'trickledown theory'. This premise continues to be the *moolmantra* of the development model operating even to date.

Gandhi's passionate defense of his educational vision was rooted primarily in common sense, life experience and, above all, intuition. He did not have access to the tools of either economic or educational theory. In contrast, the then ruling Congress Party's vision had the logic of history and economics on its side. The conflict has been interpreted as "a domain of rationality and a domain of unreason, a domain of science and a domain of faith, a domain of organisation and a domain of spontaneity. But it was a rational understanding which, by the very act of its recognition of the Other, also effaced the Other.[14]" The outcome may be seen as the "triumph of the politics of the elite over the politics of the subaltern classes."

The final word from history is yet to come. Six decades after independence, the Indian masses continue to struggle for development and justice to "trickle down". While not discounting either rationality or theory, we have now sufficient reason to inquire whether there could be a defining limit to either or both. Gandhi may not have any rational claim to be right but - in view of the global warming, climate change, rising global inequalities and socio-political tensions and cycles of crises in capitalism - history stands testimony that he was not entirely wrong either.

As the neo-liberal policies are ruthlessly pushed, the struggle between the oppressed masses and the ruling classes intensifies. The crisis has worsened in recent years. Today, 'the Neo-liberal Capitalism is riding piggy-back on the *Hindu Rashtra* forces', with the Indian polity essentially becoming a silent helpless witness. The experience of exploring and re-assessing Gandhi and his ideas on education during the course of this essay as a part of the series to commemorate Gandhi on his 150th birth anniversary has rekindled faith that the logic of history may still be on the side of Gandhian common sense, life experience and intuition. Hopefully, in the process, we have revealed the potentiality of *Nai Taleem* to act as a strategic tool of *satyagrah* for transforming the 'transfer of power' in 1947 into true and long-awaited *Hind Swaraj*!

[14] Citation by Fagg (2002) from Prof. Partha Chatterjee's *Nationalist Thought and the Colonial World – A Derivative Discourse?* (1986).

References

Ambedkar, B. R. (1936), Annihilation of Caste, Critical Quest, New Delhi, 2007.

Bhattacharyya, Sabyasachi (1997), *The Mahatma and the Poet*, National Book Trust, India, New Delhi.

Dewey, John (1907), *The School and Society*, Aakar Books (Indian Edition), Delhi, 2008.

Fagg, Henry (2002), *Back to the Sources: A Study of Gandhi's Basic Education*, National Book Trust, New Delhi.

Gandhi, M.K. (1909), *Hind Swaraj or Indian Home Rule*, Navajivan Publishing House, Ahmedabad, 1939.

Govt. of India (2009), *The Right of Children to Free and Compulsory Education Act, 2009* (No. 35 of 2009), The Gazette of India (Extraordinary), Part II, Section I, 27 August 2009.

Hindustani Talimi Sangh (1957), *Aath Salon ka Sampoorna Shikshakram*, Sewagram, Wardha, Maharashtra.

Ilaiah, Kancha (2007), *Turning the Pot, Tilling the Land: Dignity of Labour in Our Times*, Navayana Publishing, New Delhi.

Kumar, Krishna (2005), *Political Agenda of Education*, Sage Publication, New Delhi.

Mukherjee, Aditya (2002), *Imperialism, Nationalism and the Making of the Indian Capitalist Class*, 1920–47, Sage Publications, New Delhi.

Naik, J.P. (1979), *The Education Commission and After*, A.P.H. Publishing Corporation, New Delhi, 1997.

National Council of Educational Research and Training (1998), *Gandhi on Education*, NCERT, New Delhi.

National Council of Educational Research and Training (2007), *National Focus Group Position Paper on 'Work and Education'*, NCERT, New Delhi.

Parel, Anthony J. (1997), *Gandhi: Hind Swaraj and Other Writings*, Edited by Anthony J. Parel, Cambridge University Press, U. K.

Phule, Jotirao Govindrao (1882), *Memorial Addressed to the Education Commission, 19 October 1882*, in 'Selected Writings of Jotirao Phule', G. P. Deshpande Ed., *Left* Word Books, New Delhi, 2002, pp. 101–112.

Richards, Glyn (2001), *Gandhi's Philosophy of Education*, New Delhi: Oxford University Press.

Sadgopal, Anil (2010a), *The Neo-liberal Assault on India's Education System*, in 'The World Bank in India – Undermining Sovereignty, Distorting Development', Kelley, Michele & D'Souza, Deepika Eds., Orient Black Swan Pvt. Ltd., New Delhi, pp. 296–313.

Sadgopal, Anil (2010b), Right to Education vs. Right to Education Act, *Social Scientist*, New Delhi, Vol. 38/Nos. 9–12, September-December 2010, pp. 17–50.

2

Education in Modern Indian Social Thought: Educational Ideas from Gandhi and Tagore's Perspective

Arushi Kaushik

Introduction

Dewey (2004; 11) perceives education as "a fostering... nurturing... cultivating process. It is the process through which the newly heedless members of society are introduced, socialised and cultivated into fully formed members of society through the transfer of knowledge". This is not to say that education is the only means to attain membership of any society. However, it is one of the primary institutions that has played and continues to play a very crucial role in the construction, deconstruction and reconstruction of social norms through its own transformation or sustenance. Even some of the most influential modern thinkers of the Indian society have spent a great deal of time and energy reflecting on the kind of education system that prevailed in India. Any discussion on the national and political discourse of India during and in the aftermath of the colonial rule would be incomplete without mentioning the names of great thinkers and educationists such as Rabindranath Tagore and Mohandas Karamchand Gandhi. Political and social philosophers like Gandhi and Tagore, engaged with several complicated concepts that evolved under the British rule and problematised the form, the working and the undisputed ideals of the education system. Sabyasachi Bhattacharya (1997; 10) put together the letters that were exchanged between the 'Mahatma and the Poet' which began when "Mahatma Gandhi along with the students of his Phoenix School in South Africa visited Tagore's Santiniketan" (ibid). As the letters and other works of the two pioneering figures in the field of education indicate, they had rather divergent viewpoints. However, a common thread which united them was their constant reference to the questions of freedom, nationality, culture, tradition and modernity, which becomes the underlying principle behind their educational ideals. The views of Tagore and Gandhi on various matters might not have found a converging point, but the cordial acceptance of both, with respect to their right to differ led to a persistent but constructive debate among them. A very striking example of this is Tagore's address to Gandhi in order to welcome him to Santiniketan in 1940 wherein he hopefully expressed his desire for the "eternal values" of their true endeavour to be revealed beyond "the moral confusions" of their distracted politics (Bhattacharya, 1997; 25).

Contextualising the Ideas of Gandhi and Tagore in the Realm of Education

Before understanding the philosophy of education that Tagore or Gandhi adhered to, it is essential to understand the manner in which they were educated and also the context of their writings. As Kumar (2015; 132) points out in the modern Indian nation of the nineteenth century, the educated class of Indians were usually the "products of a dual education and lived in two worlds." While one section of Indians was educated in missionary schools, another section was homeschooled. The curriculum centred around "learning of Indian languages; their mastering of indigenous narratives, epistemologies, and practices" (ibid). The purpose of my paper is not to give a detailed biographical sketch of the two thinkers. I have made an attempt to briefly mention their backgrounds in order to understand the genesis of their intellectual moorings.

Tagore came from a Bengali Brahmin family. However, the Tagores' were not puritans and brought about reforms in the orthodox ritualistic beliefs that were pervasive in Hinduism at that time. Tagore studied in four missionary schools and repetitively complained about the form of regimented discipline, impatience of teachers, partial and rote learning that was advocated in the institutional space of his schools. His indifference towards rewards and prizes was evident through his dropping out of school at the age of 14 and leaving London university without a degree. Tagore was more in favour of a holistic education rather than a regimented one.

> *"He learnt of the values of discipline in freedom, of nature as a teacher, the incomparable importance of studying in the middle of nature rather than a city, and the heightened beauty of the sky, birds, and land when set off by Sanskrit verses and Upanishadic teachings." (Kumar, p. 134)*

Tagore was growing up at a time when there was great social as well as economic upheaval in Bengal. Kumar recalls that this was time when "poverty worsened, indebtedness increased, without corresponding changes in agricultural productivity, industrialisation, education, and social awareness." Tagore not only took up the education of children upon himself, but advanced his ideas of education as being a pleasurable endeavour through the setting up of a school in Santiniketan — one that would replace the mechanical system of education that he himself had experienced as a child. Tagore's school was not completely devoid of rules and regulations. Rather, his students followed a disciplined life by rising early, cleaning and toiling, eating vegetarian food, community service and so on. However, they were also given time for free, unstructured games, for art, theatre, music, observing and mingling amidst nature. The curriculum was not fixed, and students were not segregated according to age. They were given freedom in every sense of the term, something that Tagore felt was necessary. The ultimate aim of education for Tagore had always been the development of one's personality rather than the achievement of a degree or acquiring a job. Tagore's efforts expressed the need for creative stimulation and imagination in the process of education.

Today, when a great sense of disenchantment with education is visible among students, it becomes ever more essential to draw on the ideas and thoughts of the poet. His humanist agenda and unique method of teaching emphasised — the need to explore joy in learning and teaching, the use of real life situations and real life objects, the pleasure in observing and understanding-all these were the ideals of progressive education. Another significant belief that Tagore repeatedly stressed on was the role of arts i.e. music, theatre, dance, and fine arts. "He believed that the development of personality and the best achievements of a nation are possible only with the patronage of the arts" (Kumar, 141). A significant part of the Indian population has unfortunately restricted the idea of education to academic excellence alone. While the role of academic knowledge cannot be undermined, the role of arts remains a stigmatised field for many. A child who might be more inclined towards music or theatre is pushed into the field of engineering or medicine essentially because these fields are placed on a much higher pedestal than arts.

This brings us to Mohandas Karamchand Gandhi. Gandhi, like Tagore was highly critical of the colonial system of education which he condemned as being "conceived in error, nurtured in sin" (Bhattacharya, 1997; 127). He was critical of a system which focused on mental development and neglected manual labour. His experiments in education began "with the foundation of Phoenix settlement in 1904 and the Tolstoy farm in 1910." Gandhi belonged to a middle-class trading caste family. He too, like the poet recalled his education with distaste having had difficulty with the English language and the modes of teaching that did not provide a congenial environmental for learning. During his training in the legal profession in South Africa, Gandhi became acquainted with the "the theosophical thoughts of Madame Blavatsky and Annie Besant (Bhattacharya, 1997; 130). He also read the Bible and the teachings of Buddha and Mohammad. "His young mind began to unify the essential teachings of major religions." Gandhi's experience with racism in South Africa led him to take up the role of a leader amongst the Indian community. John Ruskin's thesis argued that "the true wealth of a community lay in the well-being of all its members, the good of the individual being contained in the good of all; that all work had the same value." (ibid, 134). This had a profound impact on Gandhi and triggered him to work towards education. Along with his engagement towards education, lay his political and ethical aim to gain independence from the colonial rule. Therefore, unlike Tagore's philosophy that completely rejected utilitarian ideals, Gandhi advocated the need for material utility simultaneously with craft.

Gandhi's Basic Education scheme was not separate from his overarching political programme. He explained his underlying ideology in Young India in 1921, that the scheme of education he envisioned would "fulfil three purposes: make education self supporting, train the bodies of the children as well as their minds, and pave way for complete boycott of foreign yarn and cloth" (Acharya,1997; 604). His focus on vocational training has been criticised as restricting for children who would not be able to explore beyond their familial vocation. However, Gandhi's main agenda to stress on the need for such training was to emphasise that literacy was not the only aim of education; rather, it was the intellectual and moral development of student which was of foremost importance. His idea was not only to encourage the students to become self-reliant and productive, but also to rid the education system of the harmful techniques of rote-learning from text-books that had been employed by the colonial education. More importantly, he believed that students would learn the dignity of labour and this would rid the Indian population of the social barriers that had created blocks in their minds.

Comparison of Gandhi and Tagore: Philosophy of Education

Both Gandhi and Tagore saw education as an all-inclusive process that meant holistic development rather than merely academic achievement. "Therefore, whether you take elementary education or higher education, it is not required for the main thing. It does not make men of us. It does not enable us to do our duty" (Gandhi, 1997; 83). The key point of difference between them was that the activities in Gandhi's system of education was work-focused, whereas Tagore's focus was on physical activities and playful experiences of the students.

One of the most essential and preliminary factors in their debate was Gandhi's "programme and practice of Non-cooperation in 1920–1921" (Bhattacharya, 1997; 15). Tagore was apprehensive towards Gandhi's notions of absolute boycott of anything "western". He was against an essentialist notion of India that obsessed over the faults and misdeeds of the Western civilisation. Gandhi (87) believed that "in our own civilisation there will naturally be progress, retrogression, reforms, and reactions; but one effort is required, and that is to drive out Western civilisation. All else will follow." Tagore, like several other modern social thinkers was calling for a holistic understanding of humanity rather than relying on isolationist tendencies. It is essential to point out the difference between the two thinkers in order to contextualise the foundation of their thoughts on the education system. Although the debate between Tagore and Gandhi was on a variety of issues related to the national and political discourse of the time, the scope of this paper will remain limited to their ideas on education.

There were some similarities between Tagore and Gandhi's philosophy on education.

> "Both Gandhi and Tagore were in common enterprise of building educational institutions outside of the state-sponsored system in the colonial mould. Both of them emphasised the primacy of the mother-tongue in teaching; both tried to shape the schooling system in the mould of India's culture and way of life; and both gave salience in their scheme to students' participation in the kind of creative and productive activities, which did not find a place in the conventional schooling system." (Bhattacharya, p. 36)

Nonetheless, the debate between the two with respect to the question of education began soon after the Wardha scheme (or the Basic Education Scheme), which was published in *Harijan*. Tagore was appalled by the intensity of centrality given to manual work in the scheme. He felt that this faultily focused on utilitarian purposes rather than on the development of personality which should have been the aim of education. Tagore also opposed the special kind of education for the rural poor, which would limit them to a specific vocation. Gandhi's main aim was to make the schools financially independent of the support they received from the colonial government. Furthermore, he strongly advocated the idea of intellectual training through productive labour. Thus, the objections raised by Tagore were not crucial for Gandhi.

It is interesting to note that Gandhi had become an 'Adviser' to the Village Industries Association in Santiniketan and Tagore had also requested him to become the life trustee of his university, Visva-Bharati, in 1937. Since Visva-Bharati was established outside the university system created by the colonial Government, it did not receive any financial aid or support. Tagore used the royalty he earned from his writings for the University. However, in 1935, Tagore explained the financial trouble his university was facing to Gandhi. Within six months, Gandhi sent Tagore a substantial amount which was contributed by his friends and admirers. Gandhi, however, abhorred Tagore's efforts to raise funds for the university through what the poet believed to be artistic expressions through song and dramatic performance. Gandhi believed that these were "damaging to the dignity of the poet and his institution" (Bhattacharya, 1997; 25), whereas Tagore felt that this was only an offshoot of the culture that he had been trying to build at Santiniketan; more importantly, it was a "part of poet's religion" (ibid).

It is necessary to understand that Gandhi's discourse on education was "an integral part of his ethics based political programme" (Acharya, 1997; 601). After all, he was a leader of the masses and a leader of ethical politics during the freedom struggle. Tagore's discourse on the other hand does reflect the intellectual bent of a poetic mind and is "a little eclectic" (ibid). Both were, nonetheless, constructing a discourse on education for 'free India' which is where the overlaps in their philosophical standing become clear. Gandhi and Tagore were experimenting with their schools, in the wake of the freedom struggle. This meant that the air was predictably filled with the scent of national pride. A large section of people had begun to get disenchanted with the appeal and charm of English education and Macaulay's patronizing attempt to "civilize" the people of India.

Gandhi and Tagore's Discourses on Education

"It is no wonder that both Tagore and Gandhi had started their discourse on education with a critique of the colonial system of education. An urge for building the national system led both of them to develop their educational ideals." (Acharya; 1997; 601). A large part of their discourse on education focused on the importance of using mother tongue as the medium of teaching and learning rather than the alien language of the colonial rulers. In fact, a large part of Tagore's writing was in his native language, and Gandhi, too, wrote extensively in Gujarati. Tagore repeatedly stressed the need to use the mother tongue in order to include a vast majority of the masses who were being left out of the existing system of education due to their unfamiliarity with the English language. Gandhi too believed that the mother tongue should be used as the medium of instruction up to the highest level of education. "Of all the superstitions that affect India" wrote Gandhi (ibid; 602), "none is as great as that knowledge of the English language is necessary for imbibing ideas of liberty and developing accuracy of thought."

Eventually, we see a shift, especially in Tagore's educational ideals since he was uncomfortable with the limits of nationalism that was isolationist and exclusive in its scope. Rather, he professed the need to understand education as a universalist emancipatory goal that connected the entire humanity, irrespective of their geographical place of residence. Gandhi, on the other hand continued to urge for a nativist education that denied any influence of the modern western civilisation. This point of departure is clearly reflected through their opinion on the question of English language. While Gandhi was in favour of complete rejection of English language till the child was 14 years of age, Tagore was "all in favour of teaching English as a subject, even right from the beginning" (Acharya: 1997; 602). In fact, Gandhi's radical thought is reflected when he writes that "Rammohun Roy would have been a greater reformer and Lokmanya Tilak would have been a greater scholar, if they had not started with the handicap of having to think in English.... No country can become great by producing a race of translators" (ibid).

Critical Analysis: An Appraisal

It is true that the educational ideals that were visualised and put into practice by some of the greatest educators of their time failed to get incorporated into mainstream education. It is only through the writings of Dewey, Gandhi and Tagore that one envisions a critique of the mainstream institutions, who in practice and principles have failed to attain the goals of holistic education. Gandhi and Tagore were pragmatic in their approach towards education as they emphasised upon ideas like freedom and manual labour, which was put into actual practice. Through their set of educational experiments, they redefined the idea of progressive education by disassociating it from the colonial English education. While their education emphasised upon the dexterous use of hand, heart and mind and aimed to inculcate traits such as self reliance; progressive education only focused on producing rational, regimented, docile students resorting to mechanised rote learning.

The discourse of mainstream education system in India was influenced by Nehru's modernisation plan in the wake of independence. This unfortunately went hand in hand with disengagement with the educational discourse that the poet and the mass leader's frame of mind had been striving towards. It is not surprising then that a large part of the critique regarding the current education system comes from its focus on the very principles that the colonial system of education had imposed on its subjects.

Tagore believed that it was important for the east to learn modern science and technology from the west in exchange of the rich spiritual wisdom. But is it possible to look at the east and the west in the light of such binary opposites? Most importantly, the assumption that such an exchange can take place devoid of power relations was a farfetched desire of a poet's heart that has been repeatedly questioned by his critics. Gandhi's alternative discourse which professed the idea of work based education and village-based economy was a reaction to the power dynamics that he believed would follow if India blindly walked on the road towards modernisation. However, he too has been criticised for the construction of essentialist categories that focused on only a remote aspect of the diverse Indian civilisation overlooking its complex and dynamic nature. The foundation of Tagore's educational ideals lies in his notion of Tapoban or the union between human beings and nature. He did not approve of the material utility factor that Gandhi stressed in his scheme of profit yielding manual labour. While Gandhi was looking at social revolution through education, Tagore was appealing to the spiritual moorings of universal humanism, which he felt was essential for the child to realise freedom. As Acharya (1997; 603) points out, Dewey's ideas and experiments with school education had a visible impact on Tagore who remained in close association with Dewey's student, Elmhirst. In fact, Elmhirst had a very crucial role to play in the establishment of the Sriniketan experiment. The extent of Gandhi and Tagore's influence on the mainstream education system today is remote and usually forms the curriculum of what is termed as "alternative educational institutions." However, any student of education understands the unrivalled contribution that both the thinkers have made towards this field by encouraging several leaders to look beyond the obvious, visualise beyond the barriers and create beyond the imaginable.

References

Acharya, P. (1997). Educational Ideals of Tagore and Gandhi: A Comparative Study. *Economic and Political Weekly*.

Bhattacharya, S. (1997). The Mahatma and the Poet: Letters and Debates between Gandhi and Tagore, 1915–1941. National Book Trust.

Dewey, John (2004). *Education as a Social Function in Democracy and Education*. Krishna Kumar (Ed.). Aakar Books.

Gandhi. M. (1997). *Gandhi: Hind Swaraj and Other Writings* (Cambridge Texts in Modern Politics) A. Parel, Ed.). Cambridge University Press, 1997.

Kumar, N (2015). The Educational Efforts of Rabindranath Tagore in *Rabindranath Tagore in the 21st Century*. Debashish Banerji (Ed.). Springer India (2015).

3

Revising Gandhi's Idea of Nation and Nationalism: Relevance in Contemporary Education

Bhumika Rajdev and Anamica Sharma

Introduction

Individual identity is distinct from the nationalistic identity. The idea of what constitutes a nation is debatable- whether it is one's set of beliefs, values, ideologies which go into the making of nation or a set of revolutionary movements which play a pivotal role in the construction of nation. Some theorists view nation as natural, like they always existed, while the other set of theorists maintain that nations are a modern construct. Even though there are theorists who believe that a nation is a modern construct, yet it is undeniable that it has its roots in the remote past. Steven Grosby is one of such theorist who traces the beginnings of the formation of nations to 16th and 17th century in England and 18th century in the United States and France. He attributes the construction of nations to factors like 'democratic conceptions of political participation, the social mobility of industrial capitalism, and technological advancements in transportation and communication' (Grosby, 2005, p. 57). These factors, in his view, contributed to the transformation of distinct communities into a national community.

While much has been talked and written about 'nation' as a concept and its probable history, 'nationalism' is a relatively modern concept. 'Nationalism', as a term, first emerged in the writings of the French Priest, Augustin Barruel, in the 18th century. It gained prominence again in the mid-19th century as a result of varied historical processes like the national revolution of Europe. But giving any one definition of 'nation' and 'nationalism' which can bring a consensus amongst scholars is not as easy as providing the etymology of this word because there are different approaches to defining it. As a result of complex historical factors in which the construct of nation and nationalism emerged, these terms remain problematic and contentious.

Owing to the complexities related to these terms, nation and nationalism can have dual aspects and it is important to analyse both positive and negative connotations of these. While Ernest Renan, JV Stalin and Benedict Anderson presented a positive picture of nationalism; Tagore, Ernest Gellner and Johan Huizinga highlight negative aspects of it. Ernest Renan's urged people to forget their differences based on religion, race, geography to unite for the creation of independent nation-states by overthrowing feudalism and monarchy (Renan, 1992, p. 9). JV Stalin conceptualised nation as a historically comprised cultural community and situate it in the holistic bonds which sustain when people have lived together for over a long history (Stalin, 2012, p. 8). In contrast to these theorists, Gellner denounces the idea of nationalism when it stands for the demand of homogeneity through the imposition of one's high culture on communities with low culture (Gellner, 2008, p. 7). Similar to Gellner, Huizinga attacks the nationalism of nineteenth and twentieth century which was governed by a strong desire to have one's own nation-state and impose it over others (Huizinga, 1984, p. 97).

Gandhi's idea of nation and nationalism is the antipode of contemporary nationalism. According to him, 'it is not the nationalism that is evil; it is the narrowness, selfishness, exclusiveness which is the bane of modern nations which is evil'. Gandhi wanted India to attain freedom from British colonialism and domination to be an independent nation state which has attained 'Purna Swaraj' or complete 'self-rule/ government'. However, towards the end of colonial rule, Gandhi also wanted to have a moral regeneration and that is why his idea of nation and nationalism was grounded in moral philosophy. The ideals and values such as truth, non-violence and righteousness were the cornerstone of his nation and nationalism and this, he believed, will lead the society towards harmony, peace and tolerance (Gandhi, 1909, pp. 42–43). Gandhi was a Hindu at heart but despite being a religious man, Gandhi's India was for all and his idea of nationalism was not governed by any one religion, race, or ethnicity.

If we want to pursue and understand Gandhi's concept of nation and nationalism, it is important to understand the idea of 'Swaraj', 'Ramrajya' and 'Trusteeship' given by Gandhi.

Swaraj

Swaraj means 'self-rule' or 'self-government' and can be seen from two perspectives—political and individual. Self-government means continuous effort to be independent of government control—both foreign or national. In Indian context, the word usually refers to Gandhi's concept of Indian independence from foreign domination. According to Gandhi, an ideal government is not the one which orders everything for us, thereby incapacitating the citizens of the ability to think for themselves. On the contrary, an ideal government is one that governs the least. In such a state everyone is his own ruler; he rules himself in such a manner that he is never a hindrance to his neighbour. If national life becomes self-regulated, no representation is necessary; in the ideal state there is no State and political power. Swaraj includes the freedom not of a certain number of individuals or certain classes but of the whole—the entire masses of India (Gandhi, 1928, p. 772). Self-government can neither be taken nor given. All self-government depends entirely upon our own internal strength and ability to fight against the heaviest odds. According to Gandhi, Swaraj should also be attained at the individual level which means all men and women should be self-reliant, have complete control on their thoughts, ideas, actions and build themselves in such a way that they can rule themselves.

Ramrajya

Gandhi's idea of Indian States was that of a Ramarajya. Ramrajya was not about the creation of a Hindu Raj or Hindu Nation; but about the creation of a society where all the people are treated equally. He said that, '...my Hinduism teaches me to respect all religions and in this, lays the secret of Ramarajya...'(Gandhi, 1947, p. 378). It is a divine raj where the Rama and Rahim are only one; there are no forms of discrimination and no coercion on people. Ramrajya talks about democracy in true sense; it is about the government which works equally for majority and marginalised community. In this Rajya, justice is provided to both rich and poor without any delay and the procedure is cost effective too. It follows the principle that one must not play false even with the enemy, but must deal justly with him. Gandhi's Ramrajya believed in the goodness of truth and righteousness; he wanted sovereignty of the people based on pure moral authority. The reference of term Ramrajya can be found in Ramayana, a Hindu holy scripture. This text suggests the best way of organisation and moral attitude of the society. He opined there can be no Ramarajya where inequality is rampant, where a few roll in riches and the masses do not get even enough to eat. It can be said that Ramrajya seems utopian in today's time. However, it can be seen as a concept that should inspire people to have positive goals and objectives.

Trusteeship

Gandhi viewed trusteeship as a constructive solution to poverty. His idea of trusteeship was based on the first *shloka* of Upanishad — "whatever is changeful in this ephemeral world, all that must be enveloped by the Lord; by this renunciation, support yourself and do not covet the wealth of anyone". This doctrine of trusteeship arose from Gandhi's faith in the law of non- possession and equitable distribution of resources. According to it, the person should devote everything to god and utilise things as per his need and requirement. Those people who have more money than they require, should become the trustee of people for their good. Trusteeship is rooted in the values of service and detachment, the basis of which is mutual love, trust, and care amongst people. He envisaged a father and son relation between trustee and common people; it is the job of trustees to uplift poor people. He believed in non-violence, non-cooperation and Satyagraha as a way of converting the privileged classes into trustees. Alongside, Gandhi advised poor people to be content with what they own and reduce their greed of achieving unnecessary objects. He regarded poor as less able but admitted that rich people have gained their wealth by exploiting the poor class (Gandhi, 1939, p. 145). Gandhi views this doctrine of trusteeship as the replacement of capitalism and communism. It can be applied to both the economic and household sector and can effectively resolve the economic problems of the country.

Gandhi's Idea of Education

Currently, our society is struggling with variety of issues such as unemployment, poverty, communalism, violence and terrorism. This insensitive, alienated and dehumanised nature of society can only be transformed by applying Gandhi's idea of education to current education system. Gandhi opined that we have taken life away from our education system; we can instil life into it by making it more context and experience based. His idea of education was: Education for Life, Education through Life and Education throughout Life. For Gandhi, education was a political weapon and an instrument through which he wanted to develop an ideal society. His idea of education was based on truth and non-violence. According to him, the aim of education was overall personality development of the child- body, mind and spirit (Gandhi, 1937). Gandhi emphasised 'Basic Education or Nai Taleem for all' and this principle promoted craft-centered education or education through handicraft. This idea of including manual training in formal education system was not only meant to make education and students self-sufficient, but also encourage social change and reform by emphasizing the idea of dignity of labour. This philosophy of education had an aim to provide knowledge with praxis. The role of the teacher was more of a facilitator. It denied power to the state to decide curriculum, gave autonomy to the teacher and brought a libertarian approach to schooling. Nai Taleem was based on four basic principles (Panse, 2007):

i. Education or learning in mother tongue along with handicraft,
ii. Work should be linked to the vocational needs of the locality,
iii. Learning should be linked to vocational work, and
iv. Work should be socially useful and productive.

Relevance of Gandhi's Ideas on Education

Gandhi has contributed in the political, economic and educational philosophy by giving the idea of 'Swaraj', 'Ramrajya', and 'Trusteeship'. Through the idea of 'Swaraj', he wanted a nationalist education which is free from the British control. This idea advocates for a system of education which is based on the needs, requirements and demands of our country. Implementing Swaraj in education will make students learn about the significance of being independent and having freedom of thought. It can enable students to understand and solve both the national and local issues in order to achieve social cohesion. The reforms in education system will take us towards 'Ramrajya' or divine raj of God that Gandhi envisaged years ago. Gandhi's ideal of Ramrajya in education can make students understand the importance of democracy, justice, freedom and equality for all. It can serve as the basis of providing moral education to children and develop their character by making them truthful, righteous and non-violent. For the development of egalitarian society, Gandhi emphasised on materializing the idea of trusteeship through the upliftment of poor. The incorporation of trusteeship principle would ensure the non hegemonisation of education and its availability to larger sections of society. Gandhi also opined that we can draw out the best in a child or adult if we can eradicate the 'rich-poor' division from the society.

Conclusion

The popular version of nation and nationalism is communal, jingoistic and violent; it is far from being humanitarian, accommodative and philanthropic. If this idea of nationalism is projected to students through education, it will certainly develop intolerance, hatred and fanaticism. However, Gandhi's nation and nationalism were starkly different from this dominant conception; it was more comprehensive, liberal and tolerant. While present-day nation and nationalism aims for a Hindu Rashtra, Gandhi's idea of nation was based on the ideal of '*Vasudhev Kutumbakam*'. Also, the Ram of Gandhi's Ramrajya is a complete contrast to Ram of contemporary nationalism; his nation was capable of understanding '*parayi peer*'. Thus, Gandhi's idea of nation and nationalism has the power to inculcate compassion, forbearance and critical thinking in students and transform the country into a more united, peaceful and egalitarian cohesive unit.

References

Gandhi, M. K. (1909). *Hind Swaraj*. Ahmedabad: Navjivan Publishing House.

Gandhi, M. K. (1928, June 28). *Young India*. (p. 772). Retrieved from https://www.gandhiheritageportal.org/journals-by-gandhiji/young-india

Gandhi, M. K. (1937). *Harijan*. Retrieved from https://www.gandhiheritageportal.org/journals-by-gandhiji/harijan

Gandhi, M. K. (1939, June3). *Harijan*. (p. 145).Retrieved from https://www.gandhiheritageportal.org/journals-by-gandhiji/harijan

Gandhi, M. K. (1947, October 19). *Harijan*. (p. 378).Retrieved from https://www.gandhiheritageportal.org/journals-by-gandhiji/harijan

Gellner, E. (2008). *Nations and Nationalisms* (2nd ed.). New York: Cornell University Press.

Grosby, S. (2005). *Nationalism: A Very Short Introduction.* New Jersey: Oxford University Press.

Huizinga, J. (1984). *Men and Ideas: History, the Middle Ages, the Renaissance.* Princeton: Princeton University Press.

Panse, R. (2007). *Nai Taleem: Gandhi's Experiment with Truth in the Realm of Education.* Pune: Diamond Publications.

Renan, E. (1992). *What is a Nation?* Paris: Presses Pocket.

Stalin, J.V. (2012). *Marxism and the National and Colonial Question.* London: Communist Party of Great Britain- Marxist Leninist.

Tagore, R.N. (2009). *Nationalism.* Haryana: Penguin Random House.

4

Gandhi on Education and Social Transformation: The Odishan Way

Kamalakanta Roul

> *"I had realised that one would be able to serve India in the real sense if he could serve Odisha". "The end of all education should surely be service..."*
>
> – Mahatma Gandhi (1938, 1927).

Introduction: Education and Reconstruction of the Nation

The chapter explores the tenacity of Gandhi's experiments with work-based education in Odisha. It also examines tenets of Gandhi's basic education scheme as social service and social welfare. The chapter reflects upon various moral and political components of Gandhi's educational ideals envisioned for greater social revolution and alternative way for the future of humanity. From Phoenix and Tolstoy Farms in South Africa to Gujarat Vidyapitha via Satyavadi Vana Vidyala in Odisha, Mahatma Gandhi had experimented with an important political question: what role does education system play in fostering social transformation? The principal argument of the chapter is that Gandhi firmly believed in indigenous education system that fosters social transformation not only for restructuring the society, but also for reconstructing the nation, rebuilding the ideals of citizenship and liberating the human civilisation from the scourge of modernity.

Mahatma Gandhi was a rare combination of theories and practices. He was very critical of Western modern civilisation but was also supportive of a very few moral aspects of modernity (Parekh, 1997: 78–91; Hardiman, 2003: 66–93). He had offered a bunch of original ideas, unconventional visions and tireless actions as part of his alternative modernity to the globe based on the principles of morality, equity, ecology, peace and liberation of all. Gandhi had not only pioneered a historic anti-colonial movement to liberate millions of Indians, but also provided an exemplary model of morally responsible leadership. His attempt was not just to decolonise the nation, but to lead civilisational change in the course of social transformation relying on the political principles of Swaraj, Satyagraha, and Sarvodaya. He had led the political revolution for reconstructing Indian nation from the core of society and from the heart of individual. He envisioned a strong social bonding in the triadic relationship between state, society and individual. For the purpose of civilisational change and social transformation, Gandhi effectively proposed educational ideals for character building, moral value, civic humanism, upliftment of deprived sections and social development.

According to Rajni Kothari (1988), social transformation as a theory and practice has two basic principles: modernisation and revolution. In a similar vein, Gandhi considered education as the key element of social transformation and also instrumental in restructuring and reconstructing society and the nation. Social transformation empowers people to combat exploitation, inequality and social injustice. Social and political scientists urge that social transformation has two major perspectives: teleological and empirical. In both the perspectives, education plays a pioneering role.

Teleological perspective of education facilitates the society in achieving the goals that it has set for itself. It actively works in the field of science, technology, economic growth, mitigating social inequality and character building process of citizens to make them conscientious members of democratic society. The empirical perspective of education observes the functional role of education at the ground in the course of development trajectory. Gandhi's basic education scheme combines both the perspectives and assures that social transformation represents the inevitable change in the structure and functions of society from below. It gives birth to new civilisation in place of irrational and erratic structures of society.

Gandhi believes that education is an integral aspect of society and also a way of life. It provides wisdom and logic to individual and help in imbibing civic virtue, inculcating ethical worth and enabling individuals to rationally think and rightly act over it. Moreover, self-supporting, self-dependent and independent minds are interior components of education that represents social development. Gandhi's educational ideals enumerate such kinds of components in public education system. In many ways, the New Education Policy (NEP) 2020 upholds the basic principles of Gandhian education scheme especially Nai Taleem (new education) and Gandhi's Wardha Scheme of Education (1938).

The NEP 2020 envisions that a flourishing democratic society largely adheres to public education scheme and it must be run in such a way that it can achieve highest outcome of education for the benefits of nation (NEP, 2020: 31). Truly, it is the public education that contributes to the building of nations, their growth- socially, economically, politically, culturally and technologically-and the building of a humane society (Tilak, 2020: 7). Furthermore, Kothari Commission (1964) rightly explained that education plays a decisive role in development, well being and safety of people even in the world of science and technology. The need of the hour is the educational revolution which can certainly transform the social, cultural and economic means of life (MoE, 1966, Vol.: iii, 2, 7).

Gandhi did experiment with his idea of true education as social service and welfare in many Indian provinces including Odisha. He had a very intimate relationship with Odisha and was emotionally attached to Odia people. Gandhi treated Odisha as his social laboratory for a number of eccentric experiments. He honestly admitted that Odisha was always a new learning experience for him. In spite of his repeated imprisonments and eventful programs, Gandhi paid seven visits and spent total sixty-nine days in Odisha. He planned to visit Odisha in 1922 and 1924 but failed to meet the deadline as he was jailed by colonial rule.

In the inaugural session of Beraboi Conference held on March 25, 1938 at Beraboi village, Delanga, Puri, Gandhi said, "Odisha is dearest to me in the whole of India... I am being told of the poverty and famine in Odisha since the day I landed in India... I had realised that one would be able to serve India in the real sense if he could serve Odisha. Afterwards, Odisha became a place of pilgrimage for me..." Gandhi refers to Odisha and Madhusudan Das, the founder of modern Odisha, several times in his writings and speeches. More than seven volumes of *the Collected Works of Mahatma Gandhi* (from 1932 to 1945) confirm that Madhu Babu's name has been invoked several times by Gandhi in the context of a variety of issues affecting our society, economy and freedom movement (Roul, 2021: 224).

Gandhi highly honoured few Odia leaders for their selfless dedication and devotion towards the cause of national freedom movement. They were Utkala Gauraba Madhusudana, Utkalamani Gopabandhu, Gopabandhu and Nabakrushna Choudhurys, Acharya Harihara, and Rama Devi Choudhury. Gandhi was very often getting in touch with these popular Odia leaders on the issue of anti-colonial struggle in the province.

Gandhi on Basic Education Scheme

Gandhi's emphasis over rebuilding rural economy and reinventing vocational education emerged as the alternative development model for the future human community. For Gandhi, education was an essential component for his overall political programme. He understood that politics was a process which should aim at liberating human values (Acharya, 1997: 603). Hence, Gandhi explained, education means all round development of the child-body, mind and spirit. Literacy cannot be the only objective of education. It is a means by which people can be educated (*Harijan*, July 31, 1937).

Gandhi prescribed vocational and manual training as the best method of educating individuals. Involvement in productive work will enhance the proficiency in the learning of curriculum. He envisioned that manual training was an essential part of the curriculum which can ensure self-sustaining economic worth. Gandhi's self-supporting education was an insurance against unemployment. Learning and earning are two basic components of Gandhi's scheme of self-supporting education. Gandhi suggested that providing reverence to labour, to guarantee dignified occupation and to change the means and medium of education were necessary principles of education—all these need to be imparted to children (Patel, 1953).

Gandhi exchanged his idea of indigenous education openly with colleagues and participants in All India National Education Conference at Wardha on October 22 and 23, 1937. He emphasised over mother-tongue as the medium of instruction and said that English medium education created a gulf between the educated class and uneducated masses. Gandhi urged that the Indian educated class were imparted education through an alien language, which made them ignorant of their own indigenous culture and they also survived by following the life style of their western masters. It keeps them away from the common Indians (Avinashilingam, 1960: 67). He denounced the absence of vocational training and manual training in British India's education system.

Gandhi's Nai Taleem (new education) discussed about the changes in the education pattern and the implementation of the new scheme of education especially 'education through handicrafts' (Gandhi, 1962: 74–5). It was referred to as the synthesis between vocation and education. The purpose of handicraft training is to integrate the body, mind and soul of our children (*Harijan*, June 11, 1938). Gandhi's experiments with education began in South Africa at Phoenix and Tolstoy Farms. His Ashrams were also exemplary models of vocational and manual training. In Champaran Schools, Gandhi tried his education plan of imparting knowledge on morality, civilised human behaviour, health education and hygiene tips including academic curriculum.

The basic purpose of Gandhi's education was transforming rural India, empowering poor and rebuilding the Indian nation. Gujarat Vidyapitha (1920) was exemplary model of Gandhi's experiment with indigenous knowledge, education and Indian Vedic culture. The Vidyapitha nurtured the students as satyagrahi for achieving swaraj and building the future of Indian nation.

Gandhi considered social services and welfare as true education. He worked in villages and towns, served the poor and deprived Indians. He had tremendous faith in youth, who he believed will be serving rural India for achieving 'Sarvodaya' (welfare of all). Gandhi believed that young people should teach villagers and should also work for their health and hygiene. He said that "I ask you to go forth as messengers of God carrying balm for the wounded soul of India" (Gandhi, 1947: 152).

In Gandhi's words, the basic objective of all education is to provide social service. "If any student gets the opportunity to render service to the nation while studying, he must consider it as a rare opportunity and accept this as complement not a suspension of education." (*Young India*, October 13, 1927). Gandhi's Constructive Programme was the basic political charter that had envisioned the development of the deprived sections including students, youth, farmers, tribal and untouchables (Gandhi, 1941: 25, 21, 23, 8).

Satyavadi Vana Vidyalaya, Odisha

In India, many nationalist leaders expressed their discontent over the colonial education system as it was enslaving Indians and ruined Indic culture. As a result, Gopabandhu Das's Satyavadi Vana Vidyala (1909) and Tagore's Visva Bharati Santiniketan (1921) mushroomed in India to provide an alternative Indic education system. In South Africa, Gandhi started experiments with his own ideals of education scheme at Phoenix (1904) and Tolstoy Farms (1910). Gopabandhu Das's education policy provided several combined components of education such as indigenous knowledge, humanism, rationalism, nationalism and environmentalism to his students at Satyavadi Vana Vidyalaya. Moreover, Gandhi and Tagore had offered an alternative and unconventional education system based on Indian culture and civilisation. They were critical of both western education and modern civilisation which perpetuated colonialism and imperialism.

Gandhi's basic education scheme made a departure and rupture from the Brahmanical tradition of education and proposed productive-handicraft curriculum. Gandhi remarked, "Literacy in itself is not education. I would therefore begin the child's education by teaching it a useful handicraft and enabling it to produce from the moment it begins its training...I hold that the highest development of the mind and the soul is possible under such a system of education" (CWMG, XLV: 34–35). Gandhi urged that colonial education inculcated inferiority complexity in the minds of our children and youth. It provoked them to conceive western civilisation as better and as an instrument in the destruction of the pride of their own culture. It divides the society on the basis of superiority and inferiority complex between educated and uneducated Indians (Avinashilingam, 1960: 67).

Strong reactions emerged at local levels in Odisha against the British India's education system. In 1909, Gopabandhu Das established a school at Sakhigopal, Puri popularly known as Satyavadi Vana Vidyalaya (forest school). Sakhigopal was dominated by sixteen orthodox and conservative Brahmin-settlements (Brahmana Shasana). The Satyavadi School introduced an alternative and indigenous school education. It provided autonomous and Indic education system with an unconventional pedagogical venture. Gopabandhu intended to provide low-cost school education and free access to all. It seemed that Satyavadi was sitting on the lap of Nature.

The school area was vastly surrounded with varieties of wild grass called 'bakul' and 'chhuriana' in Odia. Gopabandhu believed that, "The light of knowledge, like the physical light of the sun and the moon, should be freely shared by all, rich and poor, high and low" (Acharya and Krishan, 2010: 72). The Panchasakha (five friends) untiringly worked to run the school. Satyavadi was a synthesis of eastern traditions and western thoughts and its indigenousness was not in any way antithetical to western ideas. It was also a sort of political school, which trained the students in the ideology of Indian nationalism (Acharya and Krishan, 2010: 73). Students were also trained for national freedom movement and social service during natural calamities. The school aimed to humanise the society by inculcating moral values and sense of dedication in the students. Unfortunately, it was closed down in 1926.

Satyavadi's pedagogy was not solely confined to textbooks and classrooms. The teaching-learning method was directly connected to Nature. Teachers believed that real schooling was possible only in the open space, where Nature acts as the teacher, and becomes the main learning material (Acharya and Krishan, 2010: 72–73). Satyavadi School was running amidst trees and grasses. Regular classes were also held in the open-air space. In 1915, the school had 300 students. Teachers' common room and students dining place was operated in the open ground. The Satyavadi was also called 'chalanta' (movable) school as teachers often took the students to the nearby places for close observation of Nature. It was providing first-hand learning experiences to the students about the environment, history, culture and human habitats of the locality. Teacher Nilakantha Das who took students on outings had written famous epics like 'Konarke' and 'Mayadevi' (Acharya and Krishan, 2010:73). One of his poems 'Ramachandi re sadhya'(evening at Ramachandi) is a household name in Odisha. The 'Harihara Pathagara' was the library of the school started in a thatched house and was the only house which became concrete later. It had a sizeable collection of books and journals on a wide variety of themes and subjects in multiple languages.

According to the official report, the library had a collection of 2,388 books worth ₹6,000. In 1912, the library was set on fire by local conservative Brahmins in opposition to the social reforms undertook by the teachers-students of the school against social prejudices, untouchability, conservatism and irrationalism in the locality

During his first visit to Odisha in March 1921, Mahatma Gandhi went to Satyavadi Vana Vidyalaya to see the unconventional and Indic educational experiment of Gopabandhu. Gandhi had lunch with boarders and teachers of the school and became very happy eating food from a banana leaf. He gently suggested to Gopabandhu whether it would be possible to add a little ghee and some more green vegetables to the bland rice and 'dalma' curry. Gopabandhu politely responded, "Bapu, if these students can't make this little sacrifice, how can they withstand the rigours of freedom struggle and jail life". Gandhi was highly impressed and narrated this incident to many of his colleagues (Bhagbanprakash, 2018: 28).

Gandhi and Social Transformation in Odisha

Mahatma Gandhi was highly accepted and revered by Odia people in three different ways: as an avatar of the deity, as a savior against the oppressive British rule, and as the messiah of Odia cause. Ramachandra Guha (2008) wrote, "The people walked miles to see Gandhi, and Gandhi walked miles to speak to them" in Odisha. By 1922, Gandhi became a household name in Odisha. Many popular poems were written for Gandhi. Such a one was: "aasichire Gandhi avatara, patita tarana jagata karana, arata dharana daridra barana, dayara aadhara" (incarnation of Gandhi has come, he will liberate the depressed and will make the Universe free, he is holding spinning wheel to end poverty, he is loaded with kindness).

It was observed that Gandhi's meeting venues and retiring places turned to pilgrimage sites. Ramachandra Guha said, "Those who attended Gandhi's meetings came to see him rather than to listen to him" (Guha, 2008). The Utkal Dipika reported that Gandhi occupies the highest position in terms of popularity in Odisha which was hardly ever achieved by any Indian leader (September 18, 1920). His visits were scheduled to attain three specific purposes: inspiring Odia people to join in anti-colonial struggle; electrifying Odia masses for social revolution in Odishan society; and to set up constructive activity centres as alternative models of development (Roul, 2018). Gandhi's movements in Odisha had widely changed the socio-economic conditions of the state. Politically, Gandhi brought Odisha into the limelight of national freedom movement. Gandhi's seven visits to Odisha were not to deliver lectures to the masses. These visits were mainly based on political activism, people to people contact and *padyatra* (foot march) from village to town (Roul, 2018).

Reconnected Odisha with the Freedom Movement of India

The nationalist spirit had crept into Odisha just after the mid 19th century which resulted in the nascent of Pan-Odisha idea. It got a fillip through the press, the activities of various societies and the mushrooming of educational institutions (Mohanty, 1982: 29). In fact, the nationalist spirit awakened Odia masses with the beginning of 19th century. The

Paika Rebellion, 1904 and 1817 emerged as the first anti-colonial struggle in Odisha and also in India (Roul, 2017). The 'Orissa Association' was formed in July 1877 at Cuttack but it started working for the various interests of Odisha only in October 1879 onwards under the leadership of Gaurisankar Ray and Madhusudan Das (Mohanty, 1982).

The emergence of Madhusudan Das may be regarded as a landmark in the history of India's freedom struggle in Odisha. Madhusudan Das along with Gaurisankar Ray consecutively attended the first Bombay session, second Calcutta session and third Madras session of Indian National Congress (INC) on behalf of Orissa Association. They supported the resolutions of INC and shared it with Odia people in several meetings at different parts of Odisha. From the beginning of the INC, Odisha actively participated in different Sessions of INC. But INC was not popular among Odia people. The reason behind this was the apathy of INC towards the problems of Odisha, something which never found a place in INC's political agenda for discussions (Roul, 2018). In fact, Madhusudan Das didn't attend any session of Congress from 1888 to 1901 due to the differences with Surendra Nath Banerjee on the question of amalgamation of Odisha (Mohanty, 1982). So, Odisha politically isolated herself from the national politics of colonial India.

Pandit Gopabandhu Das poetically described the political contribution of Gandhi that, "As Bhagirath brought the Ganges to the earth; Gandhi brought the Congress to Utkala (Odisha)". Before the appearance of Gandhi in Odisha, the leaders of Indian National Congress were not bothered about the grievances and sufferings of Odisha made by ruthless and exploitative British administration. Before 1921, Congress did not support the Odia nationalist movement and Odisha's amalgamation issue was viewed as regionalism, parochialism and was against the interests of anti-colonial struggle (Roul, 2018). Consequently, Odia people turned away from Indian National Congress and focused over local issues. Gandhi's visit to Odisha electrified people's sentiment and stimulated their enthusiasm for the cause of national movement.

During his first visit to Odisha, Gandhi explained the Congress's political position in public gatherings, and propagated the idea of Non-cooperation movement in Cuttack, Bhadrak and Berhampur. *Utkal Dipika* reported that "Mahatma Gandhi now stands higher and higher having scored a triumph which was seldom attained by any Indian politician" (*Utkal Dipika*, September 18, 1920). Further, it wrote, "Orissa has accepted the principle of non-violent cooperation creed preached by Mahatma Gandhi" (*Utkal Dipika*, September 25, 1920).

Firmly Supported Odia Nationalist Movement

Gandhi reconnected Odisha with India's freedom movement which was carried forward by galaxy of committed Odia leaders including Pandita Gopabandhu. Mahatma Gandhi emphasised over the socio-economic and political backwardness of Odisha in most of his speeches delivered in Odisha. Before 1921, Congress did not support Odia nationalist movement and Odisha's amalgamation issue on the ground that it would go against the unification of India. The Odia nationalist leaders put forward the demand for a separate Odisha province on the basis of 'bhasha' and 'bhumi' (language and territory) before Mahatma Gandhi during his visit to Odisha in March 1921 (Roul, 2020: 8). He was presented a book titled "Oriya Movement" and he agreed in principle to favour the demand for a separate province for Odisha (Mohanty, 1982: 122).

Afterward, the Odia nationalist movement became an ideological apparatus of Indian National Congress in formulating policy. The Indian National Congress (INC) accepted Gandhi's policy of unification of Indian provinces on linguistic basis and demanded before the British authority to implement the policy. The Nehru government was initially hesitant to adopt linguistic states policy due to the worst experience of religion-centric Partition of India. Formation of linguistic provinces came to reality only after the enactment of the States Reorganisation Act, 1956.

Resolving the Issues of Flood and Drought

Odisha was severely affected by drought and flood in 1918 and 1919. Gandhi paid his first visit to Odisha on March 23, 1921 to catch a glimpse of the flood affected people. In a write up published in Navjivan, Gandhi desperately chased urgent help for the famine-stricken people of Odisha. In 1920, Thakkar Bapa was deputed by Gandhi to conduct the relief work in Odisha. He advised people to serve the poor people of Odisha province. On Gandhi's appeal, C.F. Andrews carried out huge relief work in the state. Jivaramji Kalayanji Kothari was highly inspired by Gandhi and dedicated his property for the service of Odisha's poor. An Ashram was built by Kothari and his wife at Bhadrak in 1927. Responding to Gandhi's appeal, Ishwarlal Vyas and spouse Purubai served poor people in Odisha and they established an Ashram at Soro (Sarma, 2008: 3–4).

Gandhi was highly concerned about the regular floods in Odisha. He invited a very famous engineer Visvesvaraya to Odisha for resolving the flood fury. Visvesvaraya stayed 12 days in Odisha and made intensive investigation of the flood problem. Finally, he didn't take his fees. Several industrialists like Ghanshyam Das Birla and Jamunalal Bajaj went to Odisha on Gandhi's request to extend their support to the poor sections. In Gandhi's Odisha Padyatra, Ms. Uma (Bajaj's daughter) and Pravabati Devi (JP's wife) took part.

Ending Poverty

Gandhi's Swaraj had political and economic dimensions. He led the freedom movement of India with the purpose of ending poverty. During his first visit to Odisha on the day of Dola Purnima, March 23, 1921, Gandhi was nonplussed while seeing the abject poverty and wrote: "Could you imagine what I saw in Odisha? I saw only skeleton-like figures awaiting death". He blamed the exploitative policies of British government and frequent natural calamities for the miserable economic conditions of the Odisha state. In Belgaum Congress session, Gandhi said, "The picture of Odisha, which is dancing before my eyes, has convinced me that it will be *Swaraj* for them, if we can provide food to them". Gandhi in a choked voice told the delegates in Ahmedabad session of the Congress in 1921 that, "All of us will be moved to tears if I narrate the suffering of the people of Odisha".

He believes that poverty can be alleviated by serving the poor. He also told that "Odisha is the epitome of poverty and if someone wants to serve the poor, he could serve Utkal". In Madras, Gandhi urged "youths to come with him to Odisha to see skin and bones around the holy land of Puri". He emphasised over agricultural growth, small scale cottage industry, production of *khadi* and development of dairy farms to make Odisha free from the clutches of poverty. In Belgaum Congress session, he said, "The best way to alleviate poverty is to propagate *khadi*. If this programme is carried out sincerely, *khadi* production in Utkal will increase and one day, this province may become the *khadi* store of India". Gandhi believed that "spinning wheel can provide food and work to the poverty-stricken people of Odisha". Further, he said, "...If this programme (propagation of *khadi*) is carried out sincerely, *khadi* production in Utkal will increase and one day, this province may become the *khadi* store of India".

Patitabana Yatra for Harijan Upliftment

Gandhi visited Odisha twice (May 5, and May 8, 1934) only for the purpose of Harijan upliftment and abolition of untouchability. He went to Sambalpur and Jharsuguda on May 5 for the same cause and addressed the gathering. On May 8, 1934, Gandhi started his Harijan Padyatra (also called Patitabana Yatra) from Puri to Jaleshwar (Balasore) for the abolition of untouchability and left the state on June 8, 1934. He visited Harijan villages during his march from Puri to Cuttack. In many places, he went to Harijan houses and advised them to prohibit intoxicants and told them to take care of health and hygiene (Nath, 2013: 567). In public meetings, he insisted that the upper caste Hindus should treat untouchables equally like own brothers and sisters and warned that 'Hinduism will be effaced altogether, if this evil is not resisted' (ibid).

Gandhi visited Gopabandhu Seva Sadan (known as Kadua Ashram) and stayed in its Harijan boarding and spoke to the Brahmins of Purushottampur who supported his mission for the abolition of untouchability (Nath, 2013: 567). Harijans were invited to dine with Gandhi and other padyatris at Satyabhamapur. During the padyatra, he used to halt and rest in Dalit hamlets, clean the area with a broom and even cleaned his own toilet that he used for himself (B. Prakash, 2018: 29). Everywhere-Anugul, Jajpur, Bhadrak, Balasore-he spoke to people against the evil practices of untouchability and organised inter-dining and inter-caste marriages among upper castes and Harijans. He advised higher caste people to eat with untouchables, help them to educate, and allow them into temples. Addressing the public at Balakati, Gandhi said, "Human vanity lies at the root of untouchability.

Like tuberculosis, untouchability consumes human beings. We must not allow ourselves to become victims of this disease. The whole world is watching us. If we do not wash this sin away, people will despise us" (Guha, 2008). During his visit to Bari in 1934, Gandhi observed that his local hosts accepted the principles of abolition of untouchability in minds and beliefs, but they were scared of Sanatani Brahmins who could raise their opposition to this. Odisha Congress leaders Gopabandhu Chaudhury and Rama Devi devoted themselves to the cause of Harijan upliftment in Odisha and became champions of abolition of untouchability.

Temple Entry Movement in Odisha

Gandhi had raised the issue of temple entry rights of untouchables in 1927 during his third visit to Odisha (Sarma, 2008: 5). He urged the trustees of different temples in Puri region to respect the untouchable's sentiment and right to worship. The trustees of Raghunatha temple allowed Gandhi to enter into it along with untouchables. In the same way, Gandhi was successful in allowing untouchables into Kunjabihari temple in Balianta. Gandhi was invited by the trustees of famous

Sakhigopal temple to see that deities wore *Khadi*. He was impressed by it but refused to go to the temple as untouchables entry was banned. The king of Puri was requested by Odisha Congress leaders to open the Jagannatha temple for untouchables.

The request was turned down by the King and Mahantas. The Mahants of Puri presented a memorandum to the Viceroy condemning the temple entry movement. Gandhi led Harijan Padyatra on May 8, 1934 from Singhadwara of Jagannatha temple Puri to Bhadrak but refused to enter into Jagannatha temple as it denied access to untouchables. In the sideline of Beraboi Conference, on March 28, 1938, Kasturba Gandhi silently visited the Jagannatha temple at Puri accompanied by Mahadeb Desai who didn't enter but was waiting outside the temple. When he came to know about the occurrence, Gandhi went on fast till Kasturba realised the mistake. The situation created a tense moment and it was expected that the conference would end inconclusively. Maulana Abul Kalam Azad succeeded in persuading Gandhi to break the fast (Nayak and Mohapatra, 2014: 30).

He didn't visit the Shree Jagannatha temple, Puri but sent a strong message to the servitors and priests reminding them how they were violating the basic inclusive philosophy of the Jagannatha culture. He further shamed the Pandas (priests) by telling when you are not allowing the untouchables and foreigners to the temple, how come you are clothing your Gods with imported foreign linen? After Gandhi's criticisms, both in Shree Mandira of Lord Jagannatha and Sakhigopal temples, the deities were wrapped up in *deshi kapada*. Responding to the swadeshi movement of Gandhi, devotees in Shree Mandira also stopped presenting foreign linen garments to the deities (B. Prakash, 2018: 28).

Facilitated Women Participation

Except some ladies of royal descent, Odia women were not taking part in politics. Gandhi's *padyatra*, village to village and town to town visits, private and public meetings for socio-political concerns deeply inspired the women community in Odisha. Women like Rama Devi, Sarala Devi, Malati Devi, and Annapurna Maharana not only gave up purdah, but also dedicatedly took the leadership for women awakening under the close supervision of Gandhi. During his first visit, Gandhi addressed forty women at Binod Bihari premises Cuttack. Rama Devi presented a bundle of hand spun threads to Gandhi in this meeting. Subsequently, a series of women leaders emerged in Odisha who devoutly contributed to the freedom movement of India.

Gandhi sought the help of Odia women for two works: boycotting and picketing. According to official records, most of the cases of picketing from Balasore and Cuttack were performed by women. Gandhi was highly impressed with Rama Devi's selfless dedication for attaining swaraj of the nation. Physician and poetess Kuntala Kumari Sabat's poems ignited women to participate in anti-colonial struggle under the leadership of Mahatma Gandhi. Her thought provoking poems 'Awhan' and 'Gadajata Krushaka' inspired people to join the movement. Protesting against the British rule at Gopalgaon, Balasore on August 16, 1946, Ashamani Devi was arrested along with several women Congress leaders (Mishra, 2019). Annapurna Maharana along with many agitators demanded the immediate release of Ashamani Devi and others and broke the police cordon. Police opened fire at the women Satyagrahi and many of them were severely injured and killed.

At the same time, Jambubati Devi from Bargarh district crossed the border of Odisha and Bihar and led a procession in Bihar. She attacked the district court of Tumuka and was arrested by the police. Jambubati Devi died in Bihar jail on July 15, 1943. She was closely associated with Gandhi and Thakkar Bapa. Gandhi totally depended on Jambubati during his visit to Jharsuguda. On January 26, 1936, Jambubati hoisted national flag at Barpali. She nurtured Parvati Giri for the freedom struggle of India (Mishra, 2019). Parvati Giri, from Bijepur, Bargarh district, was a minor girl who went to Bari Ashram Jajpur and was deeply inspired by the leaders of the Ashram. She moved from village to village and gathered people against the British rule. She gave anti-British slogans but was not arrested as she was underage. There were many women in western Odisha like Rukmani Devi Lath, and Krishna Devi who played significant role in bringing forth the message and mission of Gandhi in western Odisha.

Debating Wardha Scheme of Education at Beraboi Conference, Odisha

Gandhi Seva Sangha, Beraboi, Delanga, Puri organised its 4th Conference with the collaboration of the Utkal *Khadi* and Gramodyog from March 25, 1938 to March 31, 1938. Around 4050 representatives from all over the country participated in this conference-cum-exhibition. Gandhi, Kasturba and all his leading colleagues and leaders of Congress also attended the event till the end. All of them were staying in thatched houses and bathing in village pond. Gandhi was bathing in Budheswari pond of the village. On the inaugural day, about 75,000 people had gathered at the venue and each of them bought a two-paise ticket.

The seven days long Conference had regular speeches, discussion and resolution on several issues of the country. Important issues such as Jagannatha temple entry, abolition of untouchability, development of village economy, Hindu-Muslim conflict, health issues and education policy of the country were discussed in detail in both the shifts—morning and evening every day. On March 29, 1938, the Conference led the discussion on the new education policy of India. A resolution was passed by Kaka Saheb in the presence of Gandhi on the National Education Policy to support the Wardha Education Scheme and the recommendation of the Zakir Hussain Committee.

Taking part in the discussion, Kaka Saheb expressed his concerns over the prevalent education system of British India and Gandhi's displeasure over it. He assured Gandhi that the Wardha Education Scheme had been accepted by Congress and its government will implement the policies in their respective provinces (Nayak and Mohapatra, 2014: 159–60). There was also an exhibition of swadeshi products manufactured in homes and small-scale cottage industries of the country. The products were divided into five categories: *Khadi*, village industry, agriculture, education and health, and art and crafts.

Conclusion: Gandhi's Education Policy Paves Way for Social Transformation

Education shows the right path to individuals and makes them humans. It provides guidance in multiple ways for human and social development. Gandhi believed that education develops several moral qualities in individuals by inculcating love, tolerance, humaneness and non-violence. Gandhi's scheme of basic education emphasizes over character-building, nation-building, self-help, social service and peace. It proposes that amazing civic qualities in individuals could be developed only through indigenous and unconventional work-based true education.

Gandhi thought that his work-based and self-supporting education would be able to create the ideals of citizenship inherent in it. Citizenship rights would add more democratic flavour in socio-cultural, political and economic aspects of independent India. Basic education scheme will make our citizens efficient in understanding their problems, rights and obligation towards the nation. The work-based indigenous education will help citizens in exercising their rights and duties. Gandhi assumed that vocational education will nurture active members of society. These members will pay back to the society through their service to the nation being already a beneficiary of it. Gandhi explained that the new education venture was designed to create new professional workers who can do every essential work like manual labour and scavenging with great honour and can stand on their own feet (Avinashilingam, 1960: 15–6).

Gandhi suggested that students' community should take lead against social conservatism, preserve all good things for the nation and overcome the abusive practices of society. Students should study and debate socio-economic issues which are significant for our generation as the premier political question. No part of the nation should be left uncovered as nation-building programme (*Young India*, June 9, 1927). Gandhi very practically responded to the political question that the globe has been asking—'what is learning for and learning to' (Desjardins, 2015: 239). The famous UNESCO Report 1996 has rightly answered the question more in a Gandhian way—'learning to live together' (UNESCO, 1996).

Educational systems have two important components: transformative and reproductive (Desjardins, 2015: 239). Modern states have been facing enormous challenges in managing both the elements over the time. Categorically, India has thoroughly benefitted from the crucial role played by education in transforming society and state. It also played a central role in the modernisation process of the Indian provinces like Odisha where traditional values have been transformed into a secular rational value and survival value to self-expression values. Gandhi's social revolution in Odisha has reproduced the good and transformed the bad.

Mahatma Gandhi immensely contributed towards the social development of Odisha such as resolving flood and drought issue, ending poverty, Harijan upliftment, women's participation, temple entry movement, development of handicrafts and handlooms. In many occasions, Gandhi openly said, "he felt a deep urge to settle down in Utkala and serve the poor people of the province. He felt that Odisha's conditions could be ameliorated by selfless and full time dedicated workers with missionary zeal and spirit" (*Young India*, May 12, 1920). Odisha was a great intellectual and vocational source for Gandhi. He had honestly admitted it in many of his speeches and writings. Gandhi learnt many things from numerous sources of Odisha. For Gandhi, ideas and practices of Charakha, *Khadi*, Swadeshi economy, Swadeshi cottage industry, salt agitation, tanning industry, skill development of untouchables and labourers were first hand learning from Odisha. The practice of Charakha, *Khadi*, Swadeshi economy, Swadeshi cottage industry, salt movement were in existence in Odisha prior to the Gandhi's joining in India's freedom struggle.

Gandhi learnt many things from Madhusudan Das's Utkal Tannery and Satyabadi Vana Vidyalaya of Gopabandhu Das. For Gandhi, Madhusudan Das was the source of inspiration and Gopabandhu Das was the source of aspiration for the future India. Both Gandhi and Odisha had learnt, influenced and transformed each other immensely for attaining Sarvodaya India. Gandhi's theory of trusteeship and *daridranarayan* was highly inspired by the poverty, flood, drought and socio-economic life of Odisha. It is said that the poverty of Odisha had morally forced Gandhi to drape himself in as less clothes as possible. He gave up his Gujarati attire. He wore dhoti and used a chadar. Gandhi's walking bamboo stick (Lathi) was also a gift from Odisha presented by Acharya Harihara on behalf of the Beraboi villagers. Gandhi said 'that walking bamboo stick was the symbol of my numerous successes' (Nayak and Mohapatra, 2014: 31).

Gandhi also applied his principles of swaraj, satyagraha and sarvodaya to transform the socio-economic and political life of Odisha. He gave a distinct political identity to Odisha and he was also instrumental in political upsurge of Odisha in national politics of colonial India. Gandhi reconnected Odisha with India's freedom struggle and redeemed Odisha from political isolation. Gandhi's social service and activism in Odisha proved his proposition that true education fosters social revolution and transform the nation-building process. In Odisha, Gandhi introduced the idea of social service and welfare as the sole objective of true education.

By celebrating 150 years of the Mahatma, Gandhian scholars, social and political scientists must focus on the contribution of Gandhi to Indian provincial states. It would be a methodological innovation and a thought experiment for 'Provincializing Gandhi in India'. Probably, Gandhi was the only nationalist leader who regionalised national issues and nationalised regional issues to lead the social revolution in Indian provinces (Roul, 2020). Gandhi's role and response to regional issues has to be studied not only for broader understanding but also for exploring Gandhi's method of instrumentalizing education for greater social transformation of Indian provincial society. Such type of explorative study on Gandhi's role in Indian provinces will make him more relevant in our time.

References

Avinashilingam, T.S., (1960), *Gandhi's Experiments in Education*, Ministry of Education, New Delhi: Government of India, 1960.

Acharya, Poromesh, (1997), Educational Ideals of Tagore and Gandhi: A comparative study, *Economic and Political Weekly*, March 22.

Acharya, Pritish, and Shri Krishan, (2010), An Experiment in Nationalist Education: Satyavadi School in Orissa, *Economic and Political Weekly*, December 18, Vol. XLV, No 51, p. 71–78.

Bhagbanprakash, (2018), Mahatma's Marches in Odisha, in K.K. Roul (ed.), *Souvenir 2018, Gandhi in Odisha*, published by Gandhi Smriti & Darshan Samiti, ICHR, New Delhi and The Intellects.

Collected Works of Mahatma Gandhi (CWMG), Vol. XLV, New Delhi: Publications Division, Government of India

Desjardins, Richard, (2015), Education and Social Transformation, *European Journal of Education*, Vol. 50, No. 3, p. 239–244.

Das, M.N., (2014), Mukhabandha, in Prafulla Nayak and Ramesh Chandra Mohapatra, *Delangare Gandhi Seva Sanghara Satadina*, Published by Jitendriya Pattnaik, Bhubaneswar, second enlarged edition.

Gandhi, M.K., (1962), *Village Swaraj*, Ahmedabad: Navajivan Publishing House.

Gandhi, M.K., (1941), *Constructive Programme: Its Meaning and Place*, Ahmedabad: Navajivan Publishing House

Gandhi, M.K., (1947), *India of My Dreams*, Ahmedabad: Navajivan Publishing House

Guha, Ramachandra, (2008), Gandhi in Orissa, *The Telegraph*, February 2.

Hardiman, David, (2003), *Gandhi: In His Time and Ours*, Delhi: Permanent Black.

Harijan, (1937), July 31, 1937.

Harijan, (1938), June 1, 1938.

Kothari, Rajni, *Transformation and Survival: In Search of Humane World Order*, Delhi: Ajanta Publications, 1988

Ministry of Education (MoE), (1966), *Education and National Development*, Vol. 1, Report of the Education Commission, 1964–66, New Delhi: Government of India.

Mohanty, Nivedita, (1982), *Oriya Nationalism:* Quest for a United Orissa, 1866–1936, New Delhi: Manohar.

Mishra, Aviral, (2019), mother courage, *Orissa Post*, October 2.

MHRD, (2020), *National Education Policy 2020*, New Delhi: Government of India

Nath, Suryakant, (2013), Gandhi's Harijan Padyatra in Orissa in 1934: claims over a contested social space, *Proceedings of the Indian History Congress*, Vol. 74, pp. 564–570

Nayak, Prafulla, and Ramesh Chandra Mohapatra (2014), *Delangare Gandhi Seva Sanghara Satadina*, Published by Jitendriya Pattnaik, Bhubaneswar, second enlarged edition.

Parekh, Bhikhu, (1997), *Gandhi: A Very Short Introduction*, New Delhi: OUP.

Patel, M.S., (1953), *The Educational Philosophy of Mahatma Gandhi*, Ahmedabad: Navajivan Publishing House.

Roul, K. K., (2017), *Reinterpreting Paika Rebellion: Political Narratives of a Historical Idea of Indian Nationalism*, paper presented in two-day National Historical

Symposium on "Paika Rebellion: A Forgotten Era of Indian Freedom Struggle" organized by Culture Department., Government of Odisha, ICHR, New Delhi and The Intellects at IIC, New Delhi on October 21–22.

Roul, K.K., (2018), *Reappraising Gandhi's Movements in Odisha: Who Transforms Whom?*, in K.K. Roul (ed.), Souvenir 2018, Gandhi in Odisha, published by Gandhi Smriti & Darshan Samiti, New Delhi, ICHR, New Delhi and The Intellects, New Delhi.

Roul, K.K., (2020), *Mahatma Gandhi and Indian Vernacular Languages,* in K.K. Roul (ed.), Souvenir 2020, International Conclave on Mother Languages, published by The Intellects, New Delhi.

Roul, K.K., (2020), *Decoding Gandhian Studies*, a paper presented in two-day International Symposium on "Reflections on Mahatma Gandhi: The Global Perspective" on 4 and 5 March 2020 organized by Department of English & Gandhian Thoughts, RTM Nagpur University (MH) in association with Mahatma Gandhi Centre for Global Non-Violence, James Madison University, (VA) USA.

Roul, K.K., (2021), Decoding Gandhian Studies: The Odishan Sources of Gandhi's Ideas, in Terry Bietzel and Chandrakant Langare, (eds.), *Reflections on Mahatma Gandhi: The Global Perspectives*, Jaipur: Rawat Publications.

Sarma, B.K., (2008), Contributions of Mahatma Gandhi to Orissa: A Historical Analysis, *Orissa Review*, January 2008.

Tilak, Jandhyala B.G., A policy with many a right intention, *The Hindu*, August 3, 2020

Utkal Dipika, (1920), September 18

Utkal Dipika, (1920), September, 25

UNESCO, (1996), *Learning: The Treasure Within*; Report to UNESCO of The International Commission on Education for the Twenty-First Century.

Young India, (1927), October 13

Young India, (1920), May 12

Young India, (1927), June 9

Young India, (1927), October 13

5

Non-violence, Education and Harmonious Society: A Strategic Approach to Heal Divided Communities

Amila Rupasinghe

Introduction

The general philosophy of non-violence is the abstention from violence. It means being harmless to everybody under every condition (Sharp and Paulson, 2005). It promotes to believe that hurting people, animals or the environment is unnecessary to achieve any desired outcome. The intention of spreading non-violence is to create a beloved community. Non-violence chooses love instead of hate and teaches to forgive to restore community (Mathai, 2012). Major influential belief-systems of non-violence are Buddhism, Hinduism and Jainism (Brown, 1964; Izawa, 2008; Kotapitiya, 2015). Leaders who gave rise to the philosophy of non-violence in the recent history are Martin Luther King, Mahatma Gandhi and Aung San Suu kyi (Ralph and James.1993; Roberts and Timothy, 2009; Zaw, 2013). The two basic ideals of Mahatma Gandhi's life were truth and non-violence. He believed that truth could be realised only through non-violence (Green, 1993). Mahatma Gandhi's ideology is at par with the aims of Buddhist teachings, which is to produce an individual with wisdom to develop moral values by rational thinking leading to peace within and beyond the individual level (Rahula, 1974). Buddhist education focuses on the total development of a child's personality, which includes physical, mental, moral, and intellectual development and wellbeing (Rahula, 1974). Aung San Suu kyi does not hold to non-violence only for moral reasons, but also for social and political reasons, which led to a decade long fight for freedom of her nation from alleged military rule (Whitney, 2008). Martin Luther King explained the philosophy and practice of non-violence through six basic principles:

(i) Non-violence is a way of life for courageous people.
(ii) It seeks to win friendship and understanding.
(iii) It seeks to defeat injustice, not people.
(iv) Non-violence holds that suffering can educate and transform.
(v) It chooses love instead of hate.
(vi) Non-violence believes that the universe is on the side of justice (King Jr, 2019).

Nonetheless, these examples of the practice of non-violence in the 20th Century provides ample evidence for its effectiveness, resilience and universality, as against numerous violent power struggles from the World War I to Gulf Wars, which occurred in the same century (Pandia, 2017; Subedi, 2003).

The community is made by individuals. In a harmonious community, every member should work themselves to maintain a consistent state of inner harmony and balance (Han, 2008). The community cannot be considered as harmonious if it is inherently unjust or does not treat all the members equally by providing equal opportunities. Social harmony can be achieved when the members of society live together keeping healthy interpersonal relationships in a friendly and cordial manner (Jenkins, 2002).

Education contributes the most significant part in creating social harmony in a sustainable pattern through positive influence (Muller, 2002). Further, from sociological perspective, schools can help foster a sense of community. However, concepts for the management of violence-based conflicts would not be as straightforward as Mathematics, English or Geography to be placed in the contemporary school curriculum, which mainly targets transmitting knowledge, with a little or no emphasis on teaching to develop the moral values. (Daily Mirror, 2018). Therefore, an effective strategic approach is required to introduce moral values such as non-violence to the students at schools.

Education Approaches for Nonviolent and Harmonious Society in Sri Lankan Context

Sri Lanka has suffered from civil war for a long period in the near past. In Sri Lankan context, terms such as community harmony, ethnic harmony and social harmony are commonly used with unity and national reconciliation (UGC, 2002). The definition of social harmony, provided by the Ministry of National language and social integration in Sri Lanka is the "peaceful interaction among members of social groups". Based on this, teaching social harmony is essential for maintaining healthy relationships as well as awareness and interaction amongst people. Therefore, every field of education in Sri Lanka started to include programmes related to social harmony.

1. University Grant Commission (UGC) and the Ministry of Higher Education commenced a social harmony programme in the university level in 2002(UGC, 2002).
    - Included ethnic cohesion, social harmony, and peace education in university curriculum.
    - Taught other languages (Tamil to Sinhala students and Sinhala to Tamil students).
    - Conducted different Cultural festivals in universities.
2. 'Education for Conflict Resolution' (ECR) programme was launched by the government of Sri Lanka with the help of UNICEF in order to teach children non-violent ways of resolving disputes (How Sri Lanka educates children for peace, (unicef.org)).
    - Trained resource persons at the National Institute of Education to practise different forms of conflict resolution being used in other countries.
    - Developed methods which are appropriate to Sri Lanka (Meditation in Hinduism and Buddhism)
    - Produced ten training manuals for principals, teacher trainers, teachers and pupils, which are appropriate for Sri Lanka
    - Created a sense of inner peace, calm, and concentrated mind by promoting meditation.
    - Taught skills such as decision-making and conflict resolution for primary schoolchildren.
3. Introduced 'Peace education' by UNICEF to promote knowledge, skills, attitudes, and values to prevent violence and to resolve conflict peacefully (UNICEF 1999: I; MOE & UNICEF Sri Lanka, 1996) Accordingly, the International Bureau of Education at

UNESCO regards the pillar 'learning to live together' as a framework concept for peace education, including various topic areas such as conflict management, human rights, civic education, international and intercultural understanding.

- Ministry works with the zonal level co-ordinators for peace education, providing in-service training and funds for extra-curricular activities.
- Pre-service and in-service training which is given by the National Institute of Education.
- UNESCO's peace education guide for teachers is elaborate and widely used at the policy level.
- Organisation of inter-group meetings, the exercise of inner-peace through meditation and relaxation, care and respect for the environment and the participation of the community in peace education initiatives at schools.
- The Ministry of Education (MOE) initiated peace education in the process of primary education with the support of German Technical Cooperation (GTZ) (Herath, A,1995; NIE & UNICEF Sri Lanka; Fountain, S, 1999).

4. Under 'Sarvodaya' project, the Global Network of Religions for Children (GNRC) Ethics Education Programme has been implemented in seven selected districts in every province, engaging children representing all religious groups and ethnic groups in Sri Lanka and under this workshop on Ethics Education for Children in the seven selected districts have been completed (Heuser, A., & Koehrsen, J, 2020).
5. The national policy on social cohesion and peace education (SCPE) initiated various peace education programmes in the country and identified seven strategic areas within them — curriculum, teacher education, second national language, the whole school culture, integration, co-curriculum and research (MOE, 2008).
   I. Curriculum: Introducing Life Competences and Citizenship Education for students in grades 6 to 9; Citizenship Education and Governance for students in grades 10 to 11 and monitoring the impact of this through research and reviewing.
   II. Teacher Education: To ensure teachers are exposed to ESCP goals, developing the curriculum, teacher manuals and other materials that are used in teacher training.
   III. Second National Language (2NL): Establishment of a National College of Education for 2NL teachers to strengthen the provision of 2NL, through a clear policy on 2NL.

IV. Whole School Culture: Fostering peace and respect for rights, in the school as well as in the community.

V. Integration: Linking schools and sharing experiences through concepts like twinning, to promote further integrated schools in which every child should get a 'peace experience'.

VI. Co-curriculum: Promoting and monitoring Co-curricular activities, through various events and dialogues to promote intercultural understanding and life skills for a democratic society.

VII. Research: Development of a research network to bring researchers in SCPE together, to develop programmes and to make proposals for funding.

6. The proposals for a National Policy Framework on General Education Sri Lanka (2003) included the goals of; nation-building and the establishment of a Sri Lankan identity by promoting national cohesion, national integrity, national unity, harmony and peace (NIE, 2016).
   - Respecting human dignity through the cultural diversity concept.
   - Creating social justice and promoting human rights, duties and obligations with the concern of respecting each other.

Ministry of Education always put a great effort to set the objectives of non-violence and harmonious community under free and compulsory education system in Sri Lanka through various methods such as developing the curriculum, drawing the contents for textbooks and other educational material, setting guidelines for equality in schools, adding extracurricular activities, training teachers, etc.

Suggested Strategic Model

The strategic model to convey non-violence through education comprises of four basic schemas such as inputs, aspects, process and outputs (Figure: 1). Inputs are the direct practices such as knowledge, attitudes which were designed for practice by the target education group. Aspects are the different education levels such as early childhood, adult education which we have to address. The process is the educational programmes implemented to achieve the target output for the creation of non-violent society. Output is the identified key element- factors related to non-violence are expected to be conveyed through this process.

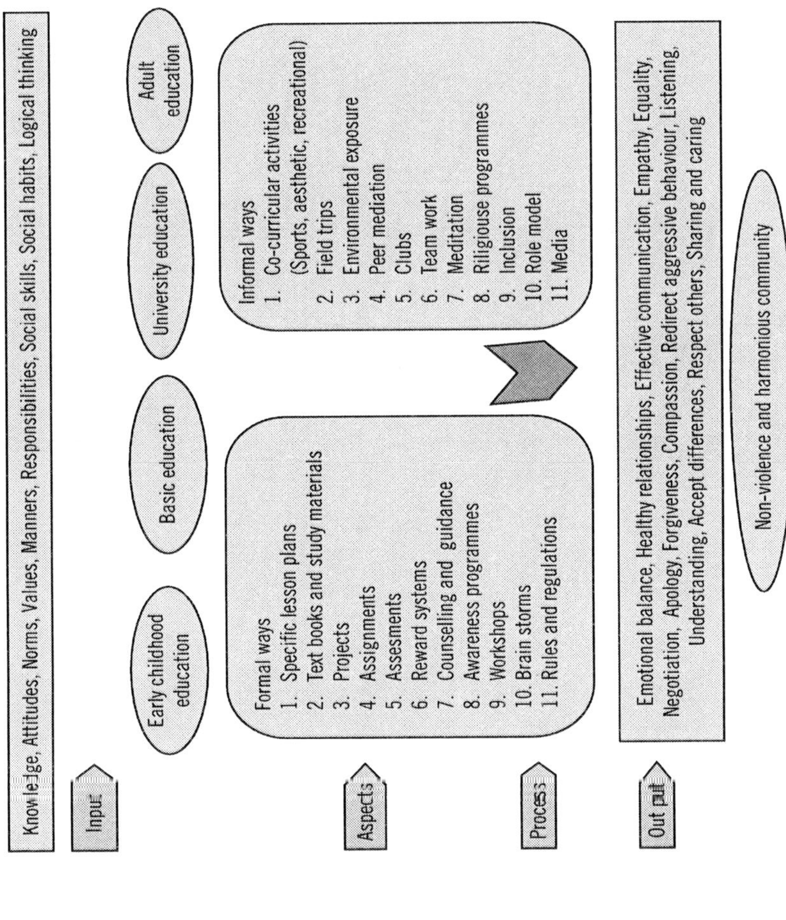

FIGURE 1. The Strategic Model for Implementation of Non-violence and Harmonious Society Through Education

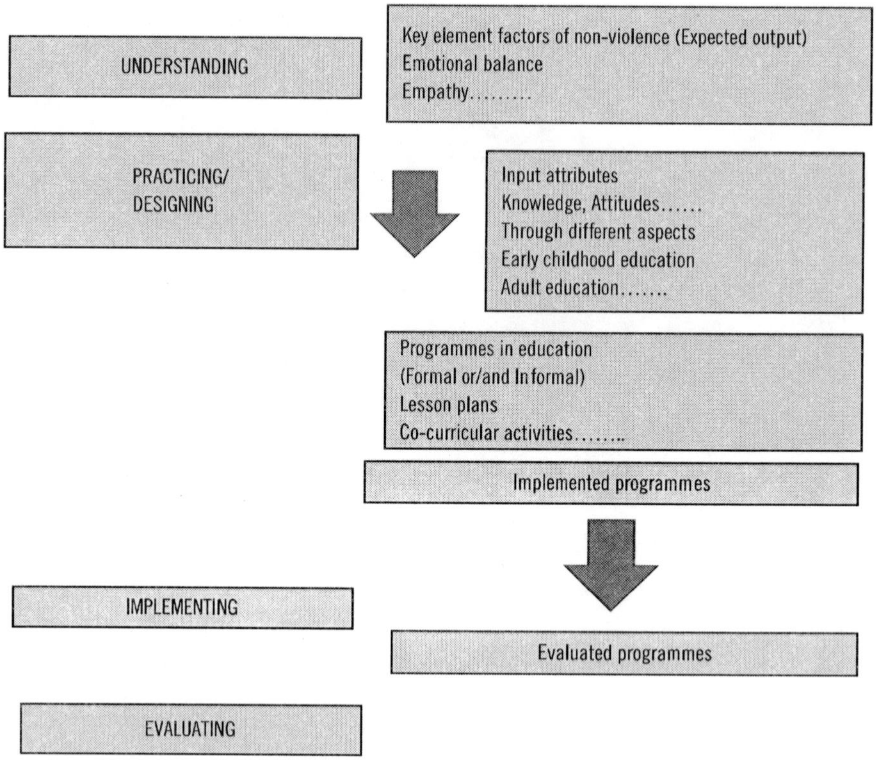

FIGURE 2. Sequential Pathway of the Strategic Model

Furthermore, this strategic approach comprises five key steps (Figure 2);

- understanding the key element-factors of nonviolence applicable for a given community;
    i. practicing and designing input attributes to improve the element-factors of nonviolence through different aspects of education;
    ii. implementation of programmes to convey the inputs linked with the identified element-factors;
    iii. evaluating the success of educational programmes on non-violence; and
    iv. Continuation/re-structuring of the educational programmes depending on the level of success.

Consequently, the strategic approach comprises a sequential pathway: Understanding-Practice-Implementation-Evaluation-Continuation

(UPIEC) of the non-violence as an essential value to be developed in each student (Figure 2). The UPIEC pathway supports students to develop rational ideas for conflict management through their own understanding of the factors leading to violence in their environment. Hence, it would be appropriate to discuss the applications of non-violence in contrast to specific violent inducing situations (e.g. family violence, bullying, racism), which would be common in the societies represented by target student groups. Further, this model provides an opportunity to refine the Best Teaching Practice (BTP) for introducing moral values through continuous evaluation of the success of both teaching and learning experience. Hence, the model itself suggests an on-going adjustment for developing teaching methods based on the experience of implementation.

Understanding the Key Element-factors of Non-violence Applicable for a Given Community

First, it is important to understand the roots of violence and arrive at the key elements of non-violence. This would result in the development of required practices, which in turn would lead to the elimination and prevention of violence. Violence from insults, rudeness to rape; murder, massacres, and terrorism is spread fast in modern societies (Narendran, 2012). In addition, the violence that is fuelled by common ignorance, often stems from the rejection of others and the fear and even hatred of differences (Lester, Jennifer and Turpin, 1999). It pits individuals, groups and cultures against one another leading to withdrawal and escalating aggression (David, 2014). In contract, the key elements of non-violence, which we expect to gain as our output in this model include emotional balance, healthy relationships, effective communication, empathy, equality, negotiation, apology, forgiveness, compassion, channelising aggressive behaviour, listening, understanding, accepting differences, respecting others, sharing and caring. The importance of key values which were listed may vary from one community to another. Therefore, it is recommended to discuss the factor/s of violence with respect to the individual experiences of the learning groups. For instance, in a society where bullying is common, equality, respect and compassion are important to be discussed in detail. Nonetheless, it is also important to make students developing a strong familiarity with the rest of the elements of non-violence, which would be applicable in their adulthood. However, these factors should be the output of our educational programmes and must be designed to foster non-violent practices.

Designing Input Attributes to Practice and Improve the Element-factors of Non-violence through Different Aspects of Education

After understanding the important key elements of non-violence to be promoted, educators should select appropriate inputs to communicate the understanding of pre-selected elements, which are of relevance to each target learning groups. It is also required to understand the attributes of the target learning group such as age; cultural and social backgrounds for designing appropriate inputs while keeping in mind our target key values of non-violence. Commonly we can take inputs such as knowledge, attitudes, norms, values, manners, responsibilities, social skills, social habits and logical thinking. These inputs can be conveyed through different aspects of education—formally as well as informally. Main aspects identified are early childhood education, basic education, university education and adult education. All these aspects should be addressed in a holistic manner.

Implementation of Programs to Convey the Knowledge and Practice Linked with the Identified Element-factors

This is the most important and challenging step in this strategic model. The programmes should be practical and applicable in real life as well as suitable for the target group. Designed programmes should have a clear focus to link with identified element factors with the target learning groups. Every programme should be designed based on clear, specific and accurate target with understanding of the audience (gender, race, culture, and age), expectations, performance level and attitudes of the group. These programmes can be presented in formal ways or in informal ways.

Formal ways include-
i. Lesson plans, ii. Textbooks and study materials, iii. Projects, iv. Assignments, v. Assessments, vi. Reward systems, vii. Counselling and Guidance, viii. Awareness programmes, ix. Workshops, x. Brain storming sessions, xi. Rules and regulations.

Informal ways include-
i. Co-curricular activities such as sports, aesthetic activities and recreational activities, ii. Field trips, iii. Environmental exposure, iv. Peer mediation, v. Clubs, vi. Teamwork, vii. Meditation, viii. Religious programmes, ix. Inclusion, x. Role Model, xi. Media

Learning programs may comprise a combination of classroom teaching, case studies, field visits to observe the consequences of violence, and most importantly opportunities for the learners to self-evaluate and communicate their experience to other fellow students.

Evaluating the Success of Educational Programmes on Non-violence

We can evaluate these programmes through simple exercises, feedback, interviews or different psychological tests as well as research work. Although the actual result may be seen after some years, we can make an approximate idea of success for evaluation. Moreover, long-term research on the effectiveness of learning programmes will be helpful in imbibing on-violence. Although programmes promoting moral values should be encouraged, but they should not lead to competition amongst students. Successful learners can be rewarded through social recognition and benefits such as leadership opportunities and awarding of scholarship. Practices such as bullying of differently abled students (blind, deaf) must be eliminated through enforcement of strict discipline.

Continuation/Re-structuring of the Educational Programmes Depending on the Level of Success

Case studies are important to explore the teaching and learning experience of the participants, and the results of such case studies should be carefully analysed for the improvement of future learning programmes.

Discussion and Conclusion

Since education plays a key role in creating a non-violent and harmonious society, we should apply some strategic and systematic methods to improve the educational outcomes through the organisation of activities and programmes. Key areas need to be identified and interventions made in those areas. The impact of relevant activities and programmes implemented in specific areas should be monitored broadly through research, and appropriate reviews. Factors leading to low productivity, social unrest, and division among the communities are more likely to be driven by elements of violence. Hence, building a strong value system is essential for the economic and social prosperity of a community (Narendran, 2012). Therefore, an attempt to promote non-violence is a lasting investment with definite beneficial results. For instance, several studies have shown that efforts to improve moral values have a strong positive effect on the economy and productivity (Surie & Ashley, 2008; Hussain & Brahim, 2006; Anderson, 1997).

Teacher education and curriculum development play a major role in integrating the learning of values such as non-violence in the formal education system. It is often challenging to introduce non-conventional subjects including moral values which cannot be assessed in a straight forward manner through grades and marks. Therefore, well-designed strategic approaches such as UPIEC should be placed to develop methods to introduce values such as non-violence. These strategic methods (for teaching moral values) should be research based in order to be result oriented. The focus of research in moral value education should expand beyond the classroom and must extend to the wider social and professional arenas. The school environment should foster a culture of non-violence through the revamping of curriculum, organisation of activities and active collaboration with international agencies.

References

Anderson, C. (1997). Values-based management. *Academy of Management Perspectives, 11*(4), 25–46.

Daily Mirror. (2018). Peace and ethnic harmony through education. www.dailymirror.lk ›news-features›

David, R. B. (2014). Six Principles of Nonviolence. *Film forecasting organisation.*

Fountain, S. (1999) Peace Education in UNICEF; UNICEF Staff Working Papers PD-ED-99/003 Programme Division of UNICEF New York. United Nations Children's Fund Programme Publications, New York.

Green, M. B. (1993). Gandhi: voice of a new age revolution. *Continuum.* pp. 123–125.

Han, A. G. (2008). Building a harmonious society and achieving individual harmony. *Journal of Chinese Political Science*, 13(2), 143–164.

Herath, A. (1995). A critical evaluation of the Education for Conflict Resolution project: A synopsis of the evaluation report. Colombo: UNICEF.

Heuser, A., & Koehrsen, J. (2020). Does Religion Make a Difference? (Vol. 20) *Religious NGOs in International Development Collaboration.*

Hussain, A. A., & Brahim, M. (2006). Administrative modernization in the Malaysian local government: A study in promoting efficiency, effectiveness and productivity. *Journal of Social Sciences and Humanities*, 14(1), 51–62.

Izawa, A. (2008). Empathy for Pain in Vedic Ritual. *Journal of the International College for Advanced Buddhist Studies, 12, 78.*

Jenkins, R. (2002). *Foundations of Sociology*. London: Palgrave MacMillan.

King Jr, M. L. (2019). Strength to love. *Beacon Press.*

Kotapitiya, R. (2015). Buddhist Studies as a Discipline and its Role in the Education.

Lester R., Kurtz, Jennifer E., & Turpin. (1999) *Encyclopaedia of Violence, Peace, and Conflict.*

Mathai, M. P. (2012). The defining features of Gandhian nonviolence. http://www.scielo.org-mx-pdf

MOE. (2008) National policy and a comprehensive framework of actions on education for social cohesion and peace. Social Cohesion and peace education unit. Ministry of Education. National Education Commission, Sri Lanka.

Muller, J. M. (2002). Non-violence in education. United Nations Educational, Scientific and Cultural Organization.

Narendran, R. (2012). Role of education in building a harmonious society: Challenges and opportunities.

National Education Commission, *(2016)*. "Proposals for a National Policy on General Education in Sri Lanka". sequel to "Proposals for a National Policy Framework on General Education in Sri Lanka" submitted in December 2003. National Education Commission, Sri Lanka. www.nec.gov.lk

National Institute of Education, Sri Lanka, (undated). Education for conflict resolution: teacher's guide for primary grades. UNICEF Sri Lanka.

National Institute of Education, Sri Lanka, (undated). Education for conflict resolution: training guide for trainers. UNICEF Sri Lanka.

National Institute of Education and UNICEF Colombo, (undated). 'Peace education activities from Sri Lanka.' UNICEF Sri Lanka.

Pandia, P. K. (2017). Role of education in peace, harmony and development in democratic system. *International Journal of Transformation in English & Education* (Vol. 2, Issue 2*) Eureka journals.*

Rāhula, W. (1974). *What the Buddha taught* (Vol. 641). Grove Press.

Ralph., &James. (1993). Northern Protest: Martin Luther King Jr., Chicago, and the Civil Rights Movement. Harvard University Press.

Roberts, A., & Timothy, G. A. (2009), *Civil resistance and power politics: The experience of non-violent action from Gandhi to the present,* Oxford University Press.

Sharp, G., & Paulson, J. C. (2005). Wagging nonviolent struggle;20th century practice and 21st century potential. *Journal of Political Science, 22(2).*

Surie, G., & Ashley, A. (2008). Integrating pragmatism and ethics in entrepreneurial leadership for sustainable value creation. *Journal of Business Ethics*, 81(1), 235–246.

Subedi, S. P. (2003). The Concept in Hinduism of 'Just War'. *Journal of Conflict and Security Law,* 8(2), 339–361.

UGC. (2002) Mission report on "Social harmony component in higher education", University Grants Commission, Sri Lanka.

UNICEF Sri Lanka, (1996) 'Education for conflict resolution project: final progress report to the U.K. Committee for UNICEF', Ministry of Education and Higher Education/UNICEF, Sri Lanka.

Whitney, S. (2008). Aung San Suu Kyi Fearless Voice of Burma: Second Edition.

Zaw, A. (2013). *The face of resistance: aung San Suu kyi and Burma's Fight for Freedom.* Silkworm Book.

6

Gandhi's Philosophy and Human Rights Education

Anamika

> "Dear Teacher: I am a survivor of a concentration camp. My eyes saw what no man should witness: Gas chambers built by learned engineers. Children poisoned by educated physicians...So I am suspicious of education. My request is: help your students become human."
>
> (Haim Ginott quoted in Andreopoulos & Claude, 1997, pp. 21–34)

Introduction

Mohandas Karamchand Gandhi (1869–1948) was not only a lawyer turned freedom fighter, but also a systematic thinker. Gandhi's philosophy of life was grounded in quotidian experiences and practices informed by a set of values. Gandhi's ideas on human dignity and its violation evolved over a period of time beginning with his first encounter with racism in South Africa. During a train journey to Johannesburg, a white officer asked Gandhi to leave the compartment even though he was carrying a first-class ticket. The compartment was reserved for white passengers. Following a brief altercation between the two, Gandhi was thrown out of the train. The painful and humiliating incident culminated in Gandhi's peaceful struggle for the rights of Indians in South Africa. Interestingly, Gandhi's endeavour in South Africa remained limited to the people of Indian origin and he did not raise his voice for the rights of the black-African population who were equally subjected to racial discrimination under the British colonial rule. Gandhi's quest for restoration of human dignity for everyone came to a full circle when he confronted social inequalities and hierarchies such as caste, class, gender and untouchability in India during the national movement. This paper discusses Gandhi's philosophy with a special focus on Human Rights Education (HRE) and praxis that can be adopted in schools by teachers to create a human rights culture. The first section of the paper is about defining Human Rights (HR), the second on Human Rights Education and the third on challenges against the implementation of Human Rights Education. The final section is on the salience of Gandhi's philosophy for Human Rights Education in current educational context in India.

Human Rights and Human Rights Education

Human Rights (HR) can be explained and understood from different perspectives, most notably moral, ethical, natural and legal. The Universal Declaration of Human Rights (UDHR) has given a simple but wide-ranging definition: "[Human Rights] are equal and inalienable rights of all members of the human family" (UDHR preamble, 1948). This definition has three important aspects. First, it considers humankind as a family and all human beings as its members irrespective of race, colour, class, speech, religion, and nationality. Being human therefore, automatically qualifies one to be a holder of Human Rights. Second, Human Rights emphasizes on the principle of equality. No one can be privileged and given rights which others cannot have. Third, they are inalienable. One cannot be denied entitlement to these rights in any circumstances.

Human Rights Education is about students and people knowing their rights and respecting others'. Much more than that, Human Rights Education addresses the developmental aspects of an individual in totality. It builds on cognition, attitude and skills required for establishing the Human Rights culture in a society. It is all encompassing in nature and attempts to reinstate Human Rights (Diallo). Koenig presented a holistic view of Human Rights Education covering economic, civil, political, social, and gender related aspects of rights and urged for equal participation by everyone so that not only the sense of claim to these rights, but also a feeling of ownership can be developed (Koening quoted in Flowers, 2002).

The domain of Human Rights Education requires special attention from scholars, teachers, policy makers and activists to fully comprehend its specific as well as general character and the context in which it is put into practice. Furthermore, by defining this concept, there is a possibility of limiting its scope too. It is a vast and limitless concept that requires a flexible outline. In other words, Human Rights Education is a constantly evolving concept and cannot be defined easily. Thus, school curricula and pedagogical processes should be immersed in the spirit of Human Rights Education rather than creating a stand-alone paper or subject to be studied without interstices.

Challenges for Human Rights Education

Human Rights Education is not a field without challenges. There is skepticism about its successful implementation. There are hostilities and intimidations from people and institutions who do not believe in Human Rights at all. For some, they are "nonsense upon stilts"- that is, the existence and practice of Human Rights Education is redundant and meaningless. Lohrenscheit (2002) raised many thought-provoking questions about Human Rights Education that is worthy of consideration:

> "1. How can it contribute to the transformation of educational institutions and education systems on the basis of Human Rights principles and democracy?
> 2. What effects can it offer, especially in restrictive or contradictory situations (for instance in schools where corporal punishment is still practiced)?
> 3. How can we ensure empowerment? And how can we prevent learners from feeling disempowered when for instance they are confronted with the many [Human Rights] violations?
> 4. How can we learn and teach about all Human Rights in an environment where they are denied. For instance, in smaller, patriarchally organised communities where women's rights are denied?
> 5. How can we on a sustainable basis integrate Human Rights Education into the existing national education systems? For instance, should it be a special course in schools or project oriented, or a general principle to be integrated into the whole curriculum?
> 6. What do we tell our learners when they know about their Human Rights, but cannot find meaningful ways to realise them (e.g. in poorer countries where even basic rights, such as education, health or housing are not fulfilled)? (p.183)."

Lohrenscheit outlined a comprehensive and exhaustive list of challenges that Human Rights Education has to address and provide solutions in order to fulfil expectations. These are the practical challenges that Human Rights Education is currently facing. Lister has also listed a number of challenges faced by the concepts of Human Rights and Human Rights Education:

1. It is too complex for immature minds.
2. It emphasises more on *rights* and undermines *responsibilities*.
3. It can take the form of indoctrination, in which the teacher becomes a preacher.
4. [Human Rights] teachers are usually more interested in social change (or in subversion) than in maintaining the fabric of society.
5. It is a culture-bound conception, born in Western Europe and North America, foisted on the world in 1948.
6. There is no consensus about what it is 'to have a right', and no consensus about [Human Rights] in general. Schools should teach only those things about which consensus exists.
7. [Human Rights] are too individualistic and private. Group rights, collective rights and the importance of the public domain are underrepresented.
8. If we arrogate to ourselves the right to pass judgment upon and seek to interfere with the internal administration of justice in other countries, we are in effect according the right of judgement and interference in our own. Nothing is worth purchasing at the price of national independence.
9. [Human Rights] issues are complex, long-term, and often intractable. Teaching about them can give students a feeling of impotence, rather than enabling them to act upon issues and outcomes.
10. Teachers of Human Rights go too far. They are not satisfied with merely teaching *about* these rights. They assert on women's rights, children's rights and animal rights. Some even talk about 'the rights of trees'. Ordinary citizens will not support this (1991, p. 252).

Together, Lohrenscheit and Lister reveal the challenges that Human Rights and Human Rights Education is facing and raise questions that need to be answered. Currently, school systems are infested with anti-Human Rights notions and practices. For instance, authoritarian nature of school; authoritarian teachers; negating pupils' views; poor communication; marks and grades seen as all-important; ultra-strict rules that tend to ignore creativity of teachers and students alike; and rote learning. These issues, questions, doubts, dilemmas and debates notwithstanding, there is no denying the validity of such an education for students in particular and for common people in general. It is a source of empowerment, an instrument to realise the dream of having a world where human dignity and worth are duly respected, rights and freedoms are enjoyed by all equally regardless of citizenship and without losing the sight and significance of responsibility in realizing Human Rights.

Gandhi's Philosophy and its Implications for Human Rights Education

Gandhi himself maintained throughout his writings that he was no philosopher, and he did not intend to propagate Gandhism, or any ism for that matter. However, his ideas are philosophic in orientation and raise pertinent questions about reality, truth, human nature, human condition, purpose of human life, and unity of man, nature and animal world. It is important to highlight that his ideas have relevance for teachers, students and Human Rights Education curriculum. The following section will explore some of Gandhi's philosophical ideas and their implications for Human Rights Education.

Gandhi and Human Dignity

Human dignity is a very vital and integral part of Human Rights and Human Rights Education. For Tarrow, Human Rights Education not only constitutes an important component of Human Rights, but also ensures fulfillment by informing people of their responsibilities towards Human Rights of others (1992). Reardon notes that Human Rights Education is social education that intends to educate for human dignity and integrity (1995). The extension of Reardon's argument can be seen in Hicks' view. He sees this kind of education as a response to take action against the dehumanisation and annihilation of people witnessed by history (1997, p. 80). Even though Gandhi used the term human dignity only sparingly, as in the quotation below, his idea of unity of man or unity of all lives is germane to it. Further, Gandhi relates dignity with non-violence or *ahiṃsā*.

> "I have known from early youth that non-violence is not a cloistered virtue to be practiced by the individual for the peace and final salvation, but it is a rule of conduct for society if it is to live consistently with human dignity and make progress towards the attainment of peace for which it has been yearning for ages past (Gandhi, 1969, p. 90)."

Gandhi makes it clear that the goal of human life is to live with dignity and non-violence. For him, every individual is respectable irrespective of birth, religion or gender. Gandhi was an obedient and dutiful child and never disrespected his parents or teachers. However, when it came to the question of physical contact with members of the lower caste, he questioned his mother's idea of considering it sinful. Such examples from Gandhi's life can be shared in the classroom as an added dimension to the ongoing discussion on human dignity. To restore the human dignity of a downtrodden was central to the thoughts and actions of Gandhi.

Right to Free and Compulsory Education

Gandhi distinguished between literacy and education. For him, reading, writing, and calculations were meaningless if these did not help an individual in becoming self-supporting.

> "By education I mean an all-round drawing out of the best in child and man-body, mind and spirit. Literacy is not the end of education nor even the beginning. It is only one of the means whereby man and woman can be educated (Gandhi, 1969, p. 151)".

Gandhi was not favourably disposed to the idea of free and compulsory education while writing the *Hind Swaraj*. Modern education was mainly colonial with a few exceptions of national institutions run by Indians and Europeans. Gandhi never believed in colonial education, as the goal of colonial education was to create generations of subservient state servants who, according to Gandhi, were not ready to play any significant role in the Swaraj movement. Gandhi was opposed to free and compulsory education also on account of economic reasons i.e.; scarce financial resources. With Wardha scheme of education (Nai Taleem/Buniyadi Shiksha/Basic Education) in 1937, Gandhi vouched for seven-year's free and compulsory education for all children across India. Gandhi strongly believed in the national system of education where the curriculum was framed according to local needs and availability of resources through the medium of instruction in mother tongue. These ideas resonate with the idea of Human Rights Education that takes into account the local context and mother tongue in order that the main ideas and content can be effectively communicated, understood, internalised, and practiced by every child. To handle the issue of scarcity of funds, as mentioned earlier, now for Nai Taleem, Gandhi proposed various mechanisms of funding that included self-sustainable craft-based education along with taxation on certain goods such as, alcohol. Gandhi's commitment to free and compulsory education for the masses is an example of commitment to Human Rights i.e.; right to education. The newly envisaged national education by Gandhi would instill self-respect, economic independence along with respect for manual labour. These match very well with the goals of Human Rights Education.

Teachers and Textbooks

Gandhi put the teacher on a high pedestal. He equated teachers with parents. Gandhi requested teachers to work along with students to make the teaching process more engaged. He gave the example of Tolstoy Farm in his autobiography:

> "On Tolstoy Farm we made it a rule that the youngsters should not be asked to do what the teachers did not do, and therefore, when they were asked to do any work, there was always a teacher co-operating and actually working with them. Hence whatever the youngsters learnt, they learnt cheerfully (Gandhi, 2009, p. 925)."

The above quotation has larger implications for Human Rights Education. It informs Human Rights educators' praxis. A teacher has to witness the growth of her/his students and groom them by participating in all activities shoulder to shoulder with the learners. When a teacher takes part in activities organised for students in a classroom, students automatically get motivated and participate enthusiastically. The involvement of a teacher not only increases the participation of students, it enhances the seriousness and accountability amongst students.

> "Of textbooks, about which we hear so much, I never felt the want. I do not even remember having made much use of the books that were available. I did not find it at all necessary to load

> the boys with quantities of books. I have always felt that the true textbook for the pupil is his teacher. I remember very little that my teachers taught me from books, but I have even now a clear recollection of the things they taught me independently of books. Children take in much more and with less labour through their ears than through their eyes (Gandhi, 1969, p. 31)."

It is clear from the above quote that Gandhi was not an admirer of textbooks. In Gandhi's order of things, textbooks remain dormant until picked up and being infused with life by teachers. A large body of teachers believe even today that a good teacher can bring any book to life. The experiences, anecdotes, and reminiscences shared by teachers with students have a longer life than the content transacted through textbooks. The textbooks can be made relevant by collating with real life experiences of teachers and students. As Lister argues, one of the challenges of Human Rights Education is that the concept of Human Rights is too difficult to be understood by immature minds (1991). Hence, presenting complex content through drab and dry textbooks would certainly put off the learners. Gandhi was trying to highlight the importance of human touch in the teaching-learning process. The nature of Human Rights Education is such that it cannot be taught through textbooks alone. The role of daily life experiences with respect to humiliation, violation of dignity, occurrences of violence in the form of capital punishment, curbs on freedom of expression, and also positive examples of respecting the rights of children and other weaker sections would have greater impact on students than a textbook enumerating Human Rights. The textbooks are indeed dormant entities that are made alive by teachers by culling out examples from real life experiences.

Teacher Training and Human Rights Education

Gandhi believed in the efficacy of teachers in the radical reconstruction of the entire educational system. A teacher is incomplete without the knowledge, understanding, and skill of a craft.

> "Only every handicraft has to be taught not merely mechanically as is done today but scientifically, i.e.; the child should know the why and the wherefore of every process. I am not writing this without some confidence, because it has the backing of experience. This method is being adopted more or less completely wherever

spinning is being taught to workers. I have myself taught sandal-making and even spinning on these lines with good results. This method does not exclude knowledge of history and geography. But I find that this is being taught by transmitting such general information by word of mouth. One imparts ten times as much in this manner as by reading and writing. The signs of the alphabet may be taught later when the pupil has learnt to distinguish wheat from the chaff and when he has somewhat developed his or her tastes (Gandhi, 1969, p. 152)."

If a teacher has been trained in a craft, her/his worldview would be different from those who is not familiar with the craft. The trained teacher's approach to disciplinary knowledge would be grounded and embedded in work experience and play the role of a bridge between school and society. The teacher training programme/institution aims to introduce every trainee to a particular craft. The orientation offers an opportunity to a teacher to appreciate manual work and thus, develop respect for dignity of labour. If a teacher is unable to appreciate manual labour, she/he cannot motivate the students to do the same. Gandhi believed that teachers should lead by example and, therefore, craft training was made essential for pre-service teacher trainees.

Fellow Feeling, Caste Inequalities and Untouchability

Indian society is inegalitarian. Powerful institutions such as caste, class and gender are based on the principle of social hierarchy. Recently, High Court of Rajasthan took a suo moto cognizance of archaic caste practices in prisons and directed the State to overhaul the prison manual. Even the prisons take into account the caste of an inmate and assign daily work accordingly. Rests of the institutions are alike. Gandhi advocated elimination of hierarchies and offered non-violent ways for doing that. Gandhi's philosophy revolved around respect for human dignity and human rights. As mentioned earlier, Gandhi firmly believed in the unity and equality of all human beings regardless of social distinction and identity.

> "I do not want to be reborn. But if I have to be reborn, I should be born an untouchable, so that I may share their sorrows, sufferings, and affronts leveled at them, in order that I may endeavour to free myself and them from that miserable condition (Gandhi, 1969, p. 55)."

Gandhi was pained to see the inhuman conditions of untouchables and disturbed by the apathy shown by upper caste people towards their plight. The caste-based prejudices and inequalities are very common and visible in schools, offices and other places, even though practicing inequality is unconstitutional and such acts are liable to punishment under the rule of law. Gandhi firmly believed that the issue of caste-based inequalities, prejudices, and untouchability could be addressed both at the level of ideas as well as praxis. Gandhi gave an example in his autobiography portraying the severity of untouchability prevalent in Indian society:

> "Even here I was face to face with untouchability in a fair measure. The Tamilian kitchen was far away from the rest. To the Tamil delegates even the sight of others, whilst they were dining, meant pollution. So a special kitchen had to be made for them in the College compound, walled in by wicker-work. It was full of smoke which choked you. It was a kitchen, dining room, washroom all in one, a close safe with no outlet. To me this looked like a travesty of *Varnadharma*. If, I said to myself, there was such untouchability between the delegates of the Congress, one could well imagine the extent to which it existed amongst their constituents. I heaved a sigh at the thought (Gandhi, 1927, p. 617)."

The meetings of Indian National Congress were occasions for delegates from all parts of India to gather at one place and interact and spend time together and understand each other well. For Gandhi, meetings of Indian National Congress were a suitable opportunity to address the issues of untouchability and go beyond it and develop harmony and respect between upper castes and lower castes and break the barrier of languages and geography.

Gandhi believed that it was through the development of fellow feeling that the hierarchies of caste could be shaken. The culture of fellow feeling had to be developed in the initial phase of schooling. The school is a meeting place of children from different castes and backgrounds. The school curriculum, including co-curricular activities should be consciously imbued with opportunities and experiences where each child is a co-learner and contributing to the learning pool of fellow learners. Children are accountable for collective upliftment of their fellow learners.

Communal eating is one way of developing fellow feeling amongst children. The mid-day meal programme is an example of communal eating where all the children of the school come together and eat the same food. Gandhi in his autobiography mentioned about the difficulties faced while running a common kitchen at Phoenix Ashram and later in Santiniketan with the help of students and teachers. He emphasised the fact that these experiments had broken the caste barriers to a large extent and inculcated a sense of service towards others. One of the goals of Human Rights Education is to respect the dignity of every human being.

Similarly, Gandhi assigned equal importance to physical exercise that was good for the health of school children as well as developed a sense of being an integral part of the school community. As seen today, all these collective curricular experiences bring students closer and develop cooperative spirit and break the barriers of caste, gender, and religion.

Gandhi, Truth and Non-violence (Ahiṃsā)

> "*Ahiṃsā* and Truth are so intertwined that it is practically impossible to disentangle and separate them. They are like the two sides of a coin, or rather a smooth unstamped metallic disc. Who can say, which is the obverse, and which the reverse? Nevertheless, *ahiṃsā* is the means; Truth is the end. Means to be means must always be within our reach, and so *ahiṃsā* is our supreme duty (Gandhi, 1969), p. 81)."

The first and foremost condition of non-violence is justice in all walks of life. A practitioner of non-violence loves everyone including those who hate her/him. Gandhi was a pacifist. He propounded an all-encompassing love that included love for enemies too. It is well-nigh impossible to love everyone equally and unconditionally. This has relevance for Human Rights Education, especially for teachers. The Indian schools are blighted, if not actually marred by physical and verbal violence. The students are robbed off their dignity by teachers and officials at school. It is not that teachers are incapable of controlling their anger. The violence occurs in schools due to multiple reasons and one such reason is deep-seated caste and religious prejudices among teachers. However, through conscious effort a teacher can conquer over her/his violent streak. Further, a logical conclusion, would be to respect and love all students. For teachers who are teaching Human Rights or otherwise, it is virtuous to love all their students irrespective of their caste or religious affiliations.

Dignity of Labour through Vocational Education

In India, manual and intellectual labour is intrinsically related to castes. Every occupation is associated with a certain caste. The occupations associated with upper castes are respected and those related to lower castes are abhorred. Although this association is getting less rigid, manual scavenging is yet to be disassociated with the lower caste. It is important to point out in this context that Gandhi included vocational training as an integral part of education. As a result, a craft oriented basic education was conceptualised.

> "This scheme is designed to produce workers who will look upon all kinds of useful work-including manual labour, even scavenging as honourable, and who will be both able and willing to stand on their own feet. Such a close relationship of the work done at school to the work of the community will also enable the children to carry the outlook and attitudes acquired in the school environment into the wider world outside (Zakir Hussain Committee quoted in Shrimali, 1949, p. 87)."

There is a tendency among the Indian upper castes to stay unemployed rather than accept a manual job. Manual jobs are ascribed to lower castes, have lower social status, and are low paid. The craft based Nai Taleem proposed to include crafts such as spinning and weaving, carpentry, agriculture, fruit and vegetable gardening, and leatherwork. The scheme of Nai Taleem emphasised the inclusion of local crafts keeping geographical conditions in mind. The inclusion of leatherwork in school curriculum was revolutionary in the sense that such a work is deeply associated with untouchables as it involves processing of dead animal's skin for making shoes and bags. Leatherwork is menial and considered impure. Purity and pollution are important elements of the caste system. The introduction of leatherwork into craft-based curriculum was an idea ahead of its time. Gandhi had himself learnt leatherwork from Kallenbach while working at Tolstoy Farm in 1912. At the farm, Kallenbach and Gandhi taught the art of shoemaking to the children residing in the farm. Thus, Gandhi was never averse to manual work whether leatherwork or even manual scavenging. Gandhi exemplified his teachings by praxis. He practiced a way of life wherein human rights and human dignity were deeply respected.

The dignity of labour is a contentious issue in India. The condition of manual workers, especially manual scavengers, is pathetic. The scavengers have to clean roadside gutters manually and many have lost their lives over the years. The newly launched government mission Swachh Bharat Abhiyan is invoking Gandhi allegorically, but the plight of manual scavengers is yet to be addressed. It is a vital goal of Human Rights Education to address the issue of dignity of labour in the classroom so that the students are not immune to the Human Rights violations that are happening in the world of manual labour.

Nation, Religious Harmony and Human Rights Education

Contemporary Indian society is struggling with communalism, an idea based on antagonism between religious communities. On various occasions, communalism confronted and thwarted the national movement. Thus, communal harmony is still the most sought-after social goal in India. Religious and communal intolerance have made way into schools and classrooms too. The inclusive character of Indian nationalism is fading and giving rise to divisive politics. Gandhi's words from the *Hind Swaraj* appear extremely relevant for the current communally volatile situation in India.

> "India cannot cease to be one nation because people belonging to different religions live in it. The introduction of foreigners does not necessarily destroy the nation; they merge in it. A country is one nation only when such a condition obtains in it. That country must have a faculty for assimilation. India has ever been such a country. In reality there are as many religions as there are individuals; but those who are conscious of the spirit of nationality do not interfere with one another's religion. If they do, they are not fit to be considered a nation. If the Hindus believe that India should be peopled only by Hindus, they are living in a dreamland. The Hindus, the Mahomedans, the Parsis and the Christians who have made India their country are fellow-countrymen, and they will have to live in unity, if only for their own interest. In no part of the world are one nationality and one religion synonymous terms; nor has it ever been so in India (Gandhi, 1938, pp. 44–45)."

What constitutes a nation? Who is a citizen and who is not? How human dignity inheres in the concept of citizenship? These are some of the questions raging in Indian society and have percolated into the classrooms as well. Gandhi made it quite clear that nationality had no basis in religion. This was an extraordinary way in which a religious person was advocating citizenship based on secularism. The evolution of a discourse on Human Rights has incorporated many issues relating to citizenship, global citizenship, and sustainable development. Therefore, it is imperative for a teacher to stress upon the inclusive nature of citizenship and its relationship with equality and human dignity. It is indeed the noble duty of a teacher to promote the Gandhian ideal of one nation and co-existence of multiple religions and sects, sometimes epitomised by the phrase- unity in diversity.

Conclusion

Gandhi can be termed a human rights advocate and activist. He believed in the efficacy of ideas when practiced on the ground. Gandhi never claimed to be a philosopher, yet raised fundamental issues pertaining to epistemology (knowledge), metaphysics (ultimate reality, truth, human existence), axiology (morals), and aesthetics (beauty). While discussing these ideas, Gandhi navigated through a perilous path to reach a destination which convinced him of the efficacy of practicing truth and non-violence, respect for human dignity, dignity of labour, and communal harmony. In this paper, some of the philosophical issues were explored from the perspective of Human Rights and their relevance for Human Rights Education. Although Gandhi did not explicitly speak about Human Rights, his ideas and strategies were deeply immersed in the spirit of Human Rights and provide guidelines for Human Rights Education. Gandhi's ideas and life set an extraordinary example for creating a Human Rights culture in Indian schools and society.

References

Andreopoulos, G. J. & Claude, R. P. (1997). *Human rights education for the twenty-first century*. Philadelphia: University of Pennsylvania Press.

Diallo, D. D. Reflections of human rights education. In L.H. Roskos & A. L. Humphrey (Eds.) *Feminism, race, transnationalism* (pp. 124–128). Indiana: Indiana University Press. Retrieved on October 6, 2009 from Ebscohost database.

Flowers, N. (2002). What is human rights education? The Human Rights Education Handbook. Retrieved on November 2, 2008 from http://hrea.org/pubs/HREA-Research-in-HRE-Papers_issue1.pdf

Gandhi, M. K. (1922). *Speeches and Writings of M. K. Gandhi*. G. A. Natesan & Co.: Madras.

Gandhi, M. K. (1935). *Young India 1927–1928*. S. Ganeshan: Madras.

Gandhi, M. K. (1953). *Towards New Education*. Ahmedabad: Navajivan Publishing House.

Gandhi, M. K. (1962). *The Problem of Education*. The Navajivan Trust: Ahmedabad.

Gandhi, M. K. (1969). *Life and Thoughts of Mahatma Gandhi as told in his own Words*. K. Kripalani (Compiled and Edited). UNESCO: Paris.

Gandhi, M. K. (2009). *An autobiography: The story of my experiments with truth*. M. Desai (Translator). The Floating Press.

Lister, I. (1991). The Challenges of Human Rights Education. In Starkey, H. (Ed.). *The Challenges of Human Rights Education*. London: Cassell.

Lohrenscheit, C. (2002). International approaches in human rights. *International Review of Education*, 48(3–4), 173–185.

Parekh, B. (1989). *Gandhi's Political Philosophy: A Critical Examination*. Macmillan: Houndmills.

Pathak, A. (2013). *Social Implications of Schooling: Knowledge, Pedagogy and Consciousness*. Aakar: New Delhi.

Reardon, B. A. (1995). *Educating for Human Dignity: Learning about rights and responsibilities*. Philadelphia: University of Pennsylvania Press.

Reardon, B. A. (1997). Human Rights as Education for Peace. In G. J. Andreopoulos & R. P. Claude (Eds.) *Human Rights Education for the Twenty-First Century* (pp. 21–34). Philadelphia: University of Pennsylvania Press.

Richards, G. (1991). *The Philosophy of Gandhi: A study of his basic ideas*. Curzon Press: UK.

Singh, N., & Kumari, A. (2012). *Educational Philosophy of Tilak and Gandhi*. Lobus Press: Delhi.

Smith, E. (2012). *Key Issues in Education and Social Justice*. Sage: London.

7

Relevance of Gandhian Values in Today's World

Ali Haider

Introduction

Gandhi believed that education alone has the power to bring out the best in individuals. He found human values such as truth, non-violence, compassion, tolerance, etc, as the basic motto of his life, which he used in words and actions. His ideals, beliefs, and values became torchbearers for people around the world. However, in order to understand the relevance of Gandhi's teachings in the contemporary context, it is essential to read his autobiography, "The Story of My Experiments with Truth". This book not only discusses the problems in detail through his theoretical framework but also emphasises on the reconstruction of society on the foundations of spirituality. Gandhi's quest for truth directed him towards discovering the universal values of life. This paper highlights some of the Gandhian values and its relevance in today's world.

Gandhi and Truth

A great detail about Gandhi's idea of truth comes from his book, 'The Story of My Experiments with Truth'. Gandhi views truth as the sovereign principle, along with numerous other principles. Truth does not only mean truthfulness in words, but also truthfulness in thought and action. In real sense, the truth is not relative but absolute and that absolute truth is the eternal principle that is; God. In this universe everything is uncertain except the absolute truth. Nobody in this world possesses the absolute truth as it is the attribute of God alone. Absolute Truth is beyond ones' own sense of perception. The truth that we perceive is, in fact, the relative truth. Gandhi' notion of relative truth is related to what we observe, such truth is relative to time and history and replaceable; what might be the truth for one might be the untruth for another. But ultimate truth is eternal and absolute, that is; above time and history. So, truth can be discovered only by one who has a sense of humility.

For Gandhi, truthfulness is most important; he not only preached about truth but practiced it in his life. The story of Raja Harishchandra impacted him so much that he questioned himself day and night, "Why shouldn't all be truthful like Harishchandra?". He further said, "To follow truth and to go through all the ordeals Harishchandra went through inspired me. I literally believed in the story of Harishchandra" (*The Story of my Experiments with Truth*, Ch.2). Gandhiji believes that only a mental scheme of truth is not enough it must be translated into thought, speech and actions. Pradhan (2016) writes, "for Gandhi, thought, action and speech form one unity because one is involved with the other". This suggests that thinking truth, speaking truth and acting truth all should be in an integrated form.

There are lots of incidents in his life where Gandhi stood for truth. One such incident is his experiment with food. Gandhiji was born into Vaishnavas family- who were strict vegetarians. He was influence by some of his friends who were meat-eaters and also started eating meat. He felt guilty about this transgression and confessed the truth before his father.

Gandhi believed that the only means for the realisation of truth is 'Ahimsa' and without self-purification, the observance of law of ahimsa is an empty dream. During the freedom struggle, Gandhi introduced the spirit of Satyagraha, a devotion to truth, remaining firm on the truth and resisting untruth in a non-violent way.

From Gandhi's point of view, people these days are running after materialistic gains. They perceive truth and reality with their senses. Gandhi claimed that such reality is merely subjective and can change over time. Gandhi advocates the quest for the ultimate truth as a way to bring peace and happiness in human lives. Now-a-days, it is common for people to measure satisfaction and happiness through their financial success. The irony is that the search for a happier self through financial success, particularly money, might become an unrealistic pursuit that is counterproductive to subjective well-being (Gardarsdottir, et. al. 2009). It is obvious that the subjective well-being is unlikely to change for upper-income and middle-income groups in economically developed countries with a change in their level of income (Diener & Biswas-Diener, 2002). Gandhi emphasised on the importance of moral values over material prosperity. For him, the pursuit of truth led to the discovery of one's inner self and the transformation of one's belief system. Gandhi's message—"the moral principal is true if it is in unison with a man's spirit, if it is close to his soul" enables us to connect with his teachings.

Gandhian Idea of Ahimsa

Ahimsa can be translated as non-violence. Gandhi was not alone who preached the message of ahimsa or nonviolence. In almost every religion, the ideal of non-violence is articulated well. Gandhi proved himself as a truly religious man and a follower of non-violence not only through his thoughts, but through his actions. Non-violence was seen by Gandhi as a means of approaching truth.

> My study and experience of non-violence has proved to me that it is the greatest force in the world. It is the surest method of discovering truth and it is the quickest because there is no other. It works silently, but almost imperceptibly, but nonetheless surely. It is the one constructive process of Nature in the midst of incessant destruction going on about us (cited in Iyer, 1986, p. 306).

Gandhi foresaw a regime of violence, which he believed was the inevitable result of modern, rational, materialistic society. His 'experiment with Truth' demonstrated that non-violence would lead a community to a more compassionate path. Through his doctrine of non violence, he rejected violence and carried out social, economic and political reforms.

Non-violence is commonly taken as a mere antonym to violence. It is regarded as not harming, injuring, killing others, but this was not exactly what Gandhi meant by non-violence. Juergensmeyer (1989) elaborated on Gandhian precept of non-violence in the following lines:

"In Gandhi's lexicon, non-violence means not only restraint from using physical force, but also the renunciation of any form of coercion. He admonished his followers even for saying 'shame, shame' to their opponent" (p. 39).

Coercion has several meanings, and two types of coercion can be differentiated in consequences as Rivett (2007) pointed: "One kind involves constraining someone against their will without the effectiveness of the constraint being due to injury or threat of injury. A child is coerced in this sense if it is carried, under protest, from a room.....the second kind involves influencing someone's conduct by hurting or threatening to hurt them" (p.45). Rivett explained, Gandhi did not reject coercion in the first form, but for the second form, in any of these senses, Gandhi is reluctant to coerce. Without any violent or even non-violent coercion of the second kind, Gandhi thought it was possible to resist injustice and oppression. Smith (1989) elaborated Gandhi's notion of coercion as a means to achieve moral ends, he explained, "if we are literally unable to prevent evil by 'non-violently facing death', we must employ coercive means, but we should at all times cultivate our own moral and spiritual discipline so as to render violence unnecessary" (p. 117). Gandhi practiced and showed many ways to combat injustice and oppression. One of the classical examples is Non-cooperation. It includes renouncing titles, boycotting government services, educational institutions, elections, refusing to pay taxes, etc. He exercised the principle of non-violence not only in India, but also in South Africa. He used non-violence as a potent weapon for uniting all the oppressed people of the world.

Gandhi's approach to non-violence seems as a solution to the contemporary global problems. Peace and harmony is compromised due to heinous activities such as lynching, murder, rape, communal riots, hate speech, etc. Another concern is that of the fake news spread by media and social networking sites which also trigger communal sentiments and induce people to resort to violence. The question that arises is how justifiable it is to blame the media houses and social networking sites, when we ourselves have forgotten the lesson which the great legend has taught us. There is a need to promote Gandhian ideals and values such as non-violence, love, truth, empathy, tolerance, etc. because surveillance and laws will not act efficiently on their own if values and conscience is compromised. There is a need to build a conducive atmosphere at our workplace and educational institutions where each person must not offend others with his or her thought, speech and actions.

Gandhi an Empathetic-Altruist

Empathy is one's ability to understand another person's emotions, feeling or conditions with a view to guide one's action. It is an interpersonal ability which aims to share the similar experiences or conditions. Broadly stated, "It is the ability of experiencing others emotions, perspective taking, prosocial concern, acting compassionately or otherwise appropriately to the situation, accurate perception of others emotions and other states" (Bošnjaković, 2018, p. 127). Gandhi was an empathetic altruist, a good companion and compassionate towards the welfare of people. The manifestation of empathy was evident in one of his journeys during the course of Champaran satyagraha. During this satyagraha, he identified with the miseries and sufferings of people, who had been suffering from several health-related issues due to their exposure to unhealthy environment and surroundings. In order to address this, Gandhi started the campaign of basic social education for the adults along with his close associates and local school teachers. This helped to improve the conditions of local people.

Moreover, in his later years, he took a pledge to wear *khadi* (a cotton fabric that was handwoven, and hand-spun) for life. He urged the people of country to boycott foreign cloth; he himself put a loin cloth over him. Seeing peasants labouring and struggling to feed themselves troubled Gandhi. He burnt his attire as he was disturbed by the fact that that the famine struck people of Khulna were dying of hunger and nakedness (Annamalai, 2014). Gandhi's talisman as seen in the NCERT textbooks (2019) is a source of inspiration for school children:

> "I will give you a talisman. Whenever you are in doubt, or when the self becomes too much with you, apply the following test. Recall the face of the poorest and weakest man [women] whom you may have seen, and seek yourself if the step you contemplate is going to be of any use to him [her]. Will he [she] gain anything by it? Will it restore him [her] to control over his [her] own life and destiny? In other words, will it lead to Swaraj [freedom] for the hungry and spiritually starving millions? Then you will find your doubts and yourself melt away."

A statement that clearly empathised with the poor and the weakest. On the one hand, it addressed the sufferings of vulnerable or marginalised, and on the other hand, it talked of the action that is intended to be taken by us for bringing about social transformation.

Gandhi while travelling to Durban, read John Ruskin's "Unto the Last" and internalised that 'the good of an individual lies in the good of all'. This later became his political philosophy "Sarvodaya"— Upliftment for all. The concept treats everyone equal regardless of caste, creed, race, gender, religion (Parathara, 2015).

From facing racial discrimination in South Africa to starting fast until death, Gandhi's journey was full of struggles. From spinning wheel as cause of dignified labour to using broomstick as an attempt to abolish inequality, all these signified Gandhi's empathy for the general masses. He also cleaned the toilets in order to empathise with the marginalised sections. He always considered the pain and sufferings of others as his own, thereby establishing a profound connect and association with the people around him. Gandhi personified exceptional socio-emotional abilities through which he led the country to success. Empathy is a significant human trait and is needed to build and strengthen understanding, create unanimity and transform thinking or beliefs. It might not be innate but can be developed or taught. Being respectful of feelings, reflecting on one's mistakes and appreciating fellow human beings and their limitations are some ways through which we can show empathy.

Gandhi identified with the pain and suffering of people. He campaigned against discrimination, untouchability, oppression and other social evils. The nature of empathy motivated him to work for the well-being of the people and the need for economic upliftment among the disadvantaged. Gandhi regarded education as an effective tool to bring social change. He considered education should be such that prepared the youth for the world. In the present day context, Gandhi's idea of empathy is visualised through inclusive education. Interpersonal relations, cooperation, teamwork, etc are the foundations of inclusive education. Such an education addresses diversity and also caters to the learning needs of the special and marginalised children.

Gandhi on Tolerance

Disagreement and discussion, controversy and dialogue are the core components of pluralistic society. Tolerance plays a pivotal role in balancing them. "Tolerance is defined as a value orientation towards difference" (Hjerm, et.al. 2019, p.899). They are of different kinds such as religious tolerance, cultural tolerance and social tolerance, etc. Sometimes, a disagreement takes a dangerous and disruptive form. Social unrest, communal tension, riots, etc are a few indicators of disequilibrium. In the past, India has seen such conflicts and protests, whether it was the war of independence or riots during India's partition.

Gandhi played an important role in reviving the power of tolerance and also in restoring equilibrium. He showed reverence towards every religion and emphasised on the unity between Hindus and Muslims. He said, "It is a fact that greater tolerance between Muslims and Hindus is needed. Sometimes one is inclined to believe that there is a greater distance between these two communities than between East and West" (26 August 1905, Indian Opinion). According to Jahanbegloo (1996), "the principle of tolerance by Gandhi thus aligns with a long tradition of Indian religious pluralism, starting with Ashoka and continuing into the twentieth century with a significant affirmation during the reign of the Mughal emperor Akbar". Gandhi practiced tolerance, fought against his weakness and ego in order to serve humanity. He showed a way for people to live in peace and be respectful of diversity. However, Gandhi's idea of peace has been thwarted by the occurrence of certain violent incidents such as communal riots, anti-Sikh bloodshed, lynching, etc. Although these events did not disrupt the spirit of tolerance, yet it gave a strong indication that people could have been primarily influenced by negative political and ideological forces. Despite turbulence and turmoil in the past, the spirit of tolerance has endured.

We can imbibe Gandhian values of tolerance by remaining true to the secular spirit of our country. Tolerance as a trait can also be inculcated in the learners by the educational institutions through receptivity, open-mindedness and following a dialogic approach as an essential part of pedagogical process. It is essential that the learners are sensitised towards accepting diversity in their classrooms-be it economic, social and cultural. This becomes the first step towards practising tolerance.

Similarly, at the societal-level, harmony can be achieved if the society demonstrates tolerance for divergent social problems such as gender roles, inter-caste/inter-religious marriages, divorce, women's rights, rights of all minorities, etc. The problems of aggression, and bullying might be resolved when people are sensitised towards values such as tolerance.

Conclusion

The values discussed above are in fact incomplete until readers thoroughly read Gandhi's autobiography and original text. These values were not only preached by Gandhi, but also practised. For Gandhi, the quest for eternal and absolute truth was the motto of his life, which can be attained by following the path of non-violence. This can never be realised by one who is not pure in heart and mind. To attain perfect purity, one has to be devoid of passion. Ideals such as non-violence and empathy bind the world together. Gandhi advocates for tolerance, acceptance and respect for diversity-regional, communal, ethnic and cultural. By embracing the principle of secularism, we as a nation have exhibited tolerance and acceptance towards people of all cultures, religion, race and ethnicity, thereby keeping the Gandhian teachings alive in spirit and action.

References

Annamalai, S. (2014, September 22). Gandhi's deliberations climaxed in Madurai. *The Hindu*. https://www.thehindu.com/news/cities/Madurai/gandhis-deliberations-climaxed-in-madurai/article6434283.ece

Almond, B. (2010). Education for tolerance: cultural difference and family values. *Journal of Moral Education*, 39(2), 131–143.

A Pictorial Biography of Mahatma Gandhi. (2007). *My Life is My Message*, Visual material courtesy Gandhi Smarak Sangrahalaya, Ahmedabad. http://www.arvindguptatoys.com/arvindgupta/e-gandhi-sabarmati.pdf

Bošnjaković, J., & Radionov, T. (2018). Empathy: Concepts, Theories and Neuroscientific Basis. Alcoholism and psychiatry research: *Journal on psychiatric research and addictions*, 54(2), 123–150.

Garđarsdóttir, R. B., Dittmar, H., & Aspinall, C. (2009). It's not the money; it's the quest for a happier self: The role of happiness and success motives in the link between financial goals and subjective well-being. *Journal of Social and Clinical Psychology*, *28*(9), 1100–1127.

Diener, E., & Biswas-Diener, R. (2002). Will money increase subjective well-being? *Social Indicators research*, *57*(2), 119–169.

Hick, J. & Hempel, L.C. *Gandhi's Significance for Today*. (St. Martin's Press, Inc., 175 Fifth Avenue, New York) d.o.i. 10.1007/978-1-349-20354-3.

Hjerm, M., Eger, M. A., Bohman, A., & Connolly, F. F. (2020). A New Approach to the Study of Tolerance: Conceptualizing and Measuring Acceptance, Respect, and Appreciation of Difference. *Social Indicators Research*, 147(3), 897–919.

Helen Riess. (2017) The Science of Empathy. Journal of Patient Experience. 4(2): 74–77. Published online 2017 May 9. doi: 10.1177/2374373517699267

Iyer, R. N. (Ed.) (1986). *The Moral and Political Writings of Mahatma Gandhi*, Vol. II: Truth and Non-violence. Clarendon Press, Oxford.

Juergensmeyer, M. (1989). Shoring Up the Saint: Some Suggestions for Improving Satyagraha. In *Gandhi's Significance for Today* (pp. 36–50). Palgrave Macmillan, London.

Krznaric, R. (2014). Empathy: Why it matters, and how to get it. Tarcher Perigee.

M. K. Gandhi, *An Autobiography or The Story of My Experiments with Truth*. (Navajivan Publishing House, Ahmedabad; Third edition 2003).

NCERT (2019). *Vistas Supplementary Reader in English for Class XII.*

Parathara,T. (2017, November). Gandhian Philosophy of Sarvodaya: A Critical Study. *International Journal of Science and Research* (IJSR), https://www.ijsr.net/search_index_results_paperid.php?id=ART20177576, Volume 6 Issue 11, November 2017, 560–562.

Pradhan, R. C. (2016). Making Sense of Gandhi's Idea of Truth. *Social Scientist, 34*(5/6), 36–49.

Rivett, K. (1988). Gandhi, Tolstoy and coercion. *South Asia: Journal of South Asian Studies*, 11(2), 29–56.

Sen, A. (2005). *The Argumentative India: Writings on India History, Culture and Identity;* Farrar, Straus and Giroux, New York.

Smith, S. A. (1989). Gandhi's Moral Philosophy. In *Gandhi's Significance for Today* (pp. 109–121). Palgrave Macmillan, London.

https://mgiep.unesco.org/article/teaching-with-empathy-and-compassion-in-schools

https://mgiep.unesco.org/article/the-need-for-kindness-and-compassion-embodying-the-values-of-mahatma-gandhi

8

Sarvodaya: A Gandhian Approach to Upliftment of All

Lata Agarwal

Introduction

History hails the dynamic impact Mahatma Gandhi's teachings and philosophy had all over the world. Gandhi identified with reality, non-violence, rationality and reason, rather than reason alone because he opined that faith originates where reason concludes (Vora, 1993). Gandhi considered truth and non-violence as an everlasting philosophy of life. There lies an underlying coherence in its apparent inconsistency. The concept of Sarvodaya accentuates the idea of independence and service to others. The Sarvodaya principle separates itself from the utilitarian aim of the 'greatest good of the greatest number', as the latter doesn't involve any sacrifice or renunciation. Sarvodaya, on the other hand, advocates for "the rise of all". (Mohandas, 1951).

Sarvodaya considers the well-being of the depressed classes like the tribal and Dalits as well as the privileged communities. Therefore, this term is also known as "antodaya" or 'rise to the last men'. Throughout the struggle for freedom, followers of Mahatma Gandhi, along with Gandhi himself, have been involved in the social activities within the ambit of "Sarvodaya". All the followers of Gandhi were actively engaged in philanthropic and political initiative of Gandhi's vision irrespective of their social class. Construction workers, who were amongst the major supporters of Gandhian values wholeheartedly committed themselves to the idea of self- sufficient village community to serve the oppressed sections of society, post Gandhi's assassination (Clements, 1983).

The basic principles of Gram-Swaraj established by Gandhi are the supremacy of man, use of all Indian labour, bread, labour, equality, trust, decentralisation, swadeshi, self-sufficiency, cooperation, "satyagraha", governance of the village Panchayat and Nai Taleem. "Swaraj" or "gram-swaraj" promotes self-government, self-control, mind control and discipline within each individual. Gandhi's ideals have often left a mark on the social and political conduct of the nation. Thus, this paper aims to explore the fundamental concept of Sarvodaya and its impact on social upliftment.

Gandhi and His Welfare Approach: A Brief Description

Narayanaswamy, (2003) described that Mahatma Gandhi has often been described as an apostle of peace who fought and died for peace. There is no doubt that the Sarvodaya movement promoted peace and tranquility. The book, "The Sarvodaya Movement: Gandhian Approach to Peace and Non-Violence" is essentially the product of the work based on the doctoral programme in the Gandhian Movement in India particularly in the context of Tamil Nadu. Illustrating the relevance of Gandhi and Sarvodaya in our daily life, the book presents an analysis of current trends among the Sarvodayites and an in-depth study in the field of the Sarvodaya Movement. Very interestingly Kumar (2017) in the document, "Gandhi's Approach to Sarvodaya", attempts to focus on Sarvodaya as one of the pillars for bringing Hind Swaraj. Gandhi's philosophy of Sarvodaya has been perceived as an instrument of consciousness raising and awareness building amongst the young with respect to their rights and duties. Primary and secondary resources were used for this document. In a similar vein Parathara (2017) also explored the world and witnessed diffusion, experimentation and implementation of various socio-economic concepts and principles from time to time through his work, "Gandhian Philosophy of Sarvodaya: A Critical Study". Parathara illustrates that Sarvodaya believes in everyone's survival and development. It is an integrated with the development of all people, regardless of class, creed, caste or religion. Rao (2018) emphasised that it is the primary duty of every citizen of India to seek the well-being of the villagers. Truth and non-violence are the two main pillars of Sarvodaya. If these two proposals are followed by all, social corruption and incongruities within the society can be rectified. It is associated with the regulation of human desires. Sarvodaya represents national integrity and dignity and condemns provincialism and regionalism. In sync with Gandhi's ideas, Sasidharan (2016) in his study reflected that

Gandhi contextualizes Ruskin in the Indian context, through his anti-industrial views, propagation of work culture and community welfare. He felt that Ruskin's values can be incorporated within the rural Indian context. Ruskin's concern depends on the last man, and Gandhi's "Sarvodaya" is concerned with everyone's well-being. Ruskin can easily be called the "father of Gandhian economic thought".

Gandhi and the Concept of Sarvodaya

The term Sarvodaya is a Sanskrit word which means "universal upliftment" or "progress of all". Mohandas Gandhi was inspired by 1908 translation of "John Ruskin's" treatise on political economy, "Unto This Last". Gandhi used the term to epitomise his ideal of social philosophy. The essence of this idea was further propagated by Gandhian non-violent activist like Vinoba Bhave, during the post-independence social movement in India. The ideals of Sarvodaya proliferated across the nation to ensure that all layers of Indian society have self-determination and a sense of equality.

The concept reflects on Gandhiji's belief of serving God by serving humanity. Sarvodaya aims at an all-round development of all, with no distinction of caste, creed, sex and nationality. The social, political and programs were aligned towards the progressive expansion of human awareness through service to the poor. The spirit of human supremacy paved the philosophical foundations of the Sarvodaya movement. J.P. Narayan attributed this movement based on the principle of "change of heart". J.P Narayan further appealed to the humankind to go beyond the materialistic philosophy of wellbeing, as social reconstruction would certainly need more than that" (Behuria, 2007).

Features of Gandhian Sarvodaya

Sarvodaya is a formidable ideology designed to intercept the socio-economic indisposition. Based on the doctrine of "Advaita Vedanta", the objective is to relinquish the systems of selfishness and altruism. Sarvodaya elucidates on thrusting the moral values into society. Truth, non-violence, sacrifice and purity, etc. were perceived to be the means to realise ethical values. According to J.P. Narayan, Sarvodaya depicts the "highest socialist values". Opposing the essence of capitalism, "Sarvodaya" represents the decentralisation of the forces of production, which encourages a mutual co-existence.

Sarvodaya holds the view of maximisation of social welfare of the people through the development of a self-sufficient village economy.

Gandhiji aimed to implement a self- sufficient economy through the practices of 'Bhoodan', 'Sampattidan' and 'Gramdan'. *Sampattidan* is a strategy for transforming capitalism into a Sarvodaya society. *Bhoodan* and *Gramdan* are strategies for agrarian reform focused on moral forces. The two movements, *Bhoodan* and *Gramdan*, exhibit ownership in the hands of the village, as well as individual cultivation by the villagers. The concepts were introduced in a bid to promote a sense of community and strengthen an initiative amongst the villagers for a self-sufficient economy. Gandhian view of the village economy through the concept of Sarvodaya focuses on reducing the inequalities of income and wealth, with the provision of self -sufficient resources, food and shelter for all. Gandhiji was a strong propagator of "villagization" and worked towards making villages as self-contained units.

Sarvodaya operates on two essential principles- that of 'truth' and 'non-violence'. If these practices are adequately applied; the society will get rid of all the ills. In reality, its realisation holds the key to rejecting provincialism and regionalism for national unity and solidarity (Varma, 1996).

Philosophical Principles of Gandhian Sarvodaya

With its origins in the Vedantic concept of the spiritual unity of life and the Gita, Sarvodaya opposes the concept of "majoritarianism", "racial class struggle" and the principle of the "greatest good of the greatest numbers". Using Sarvodaya as a means of idealism, Gandhiji condemned the state as an organisation of violence and force. Being an apostle of non-violence, he discouraged all forms of aggression. Sarvodaya reflects on Gandhiji's perceived notion of the classless and casteless society. The propagation of Sarvodaya was in response to deep-rooted socio-economic malaises, caste problems, economic disparities and social divides. Through the proposition of "Sarvodaya", Gandhiji viewed a society liberated from the encroaching social classes and a democracy without a party. Emphasis on stateless society, liberty, equality, justice and brotherhood form the crux of "Sarvodaya", which is otherwise hostile to the concept of a centralised state. Sarvodaya favours a cooperation policy, rather than the creation of a state battling against political power.

Origin of the term Sarvodaya dates back to 1904. It was used as a title of Gujarati translation of John Ruskin's book "Unto This Last". The book had a revolutionary impact on Gandhi's life, the impact of which is evidently felt in India's non-violence movement.

The realisation of happiness and the upliftment of all the sections of society is the aim of Sarvodaya. Sarvodaya ideally opposes selfish accumulation of wealth, discouraging any scope of class struggle. With the basic amenities for social harmony, 'Sarvodaya' vouches for "universalisation of self-government". Therefore, with a strong foundation of metaphysical idealism, Sarvodaya is an intellectual attempt for social and political reconstruction (Kumar, 2017).

Implications of Gandhian Sarvodaya for the Marginalised Sections of the Society

"Vasudhaiva Kutumbakam" and "Swadesha Bhubanatrayam" confirms the association of the Indian culture with the values of universal love and services. The concept of universal brotherhood, love and "service" is well reflected in the Hindu ideology of saints and visionaries. The Bhagvad Gita is replete with references adhering to the concept of "universal well-being". This concept is not only allied to the Hindu scriptures, but also with those of Buddhist and Jain scriptures. The concept of "Sarvodaya" finds mention in Jaina philosopher, Samantabhadra, even before the Christ era. Islam not only conceives Allah or God as Omniscient or Omnipresent without beginning or end. It attributes the commencement of everything from God. God's directives allude to the "well-being" of all.

Gandhi's approach to tribal development was based on indigenisation. He believed that the tribal population should be encouraged to develop an ideal village model, whose economy would be dependent on the peasants and vice-versa. Gandhians focused on the literacy programme as the main criterion for the development of disadvantaged people. Thakkar Bapa and his followers developed a social and technological welfare strategy through a network of volunteering agencies.

While attempting to comprehend tribal society, understanding their means and ways of life becomes a contested aspect; one should approach with an open mind, without interfering with the world around them. Complying with their understanding of myths and symbols also forms an indispensable parameter in understanding tribal realities (Deogaonkar, 1994).

Gandhi's association with Amritlal Vitthalbhai Thakkar, popularly known as Thakkar Bapa, shaped his opinion towards the tribal welfare. They strove to achieve the socio-economic well-being without compromising on the cultural, traditional and religious aspects of the tribal society. They collectively opted for the means of perseverance and patience to relinquish the superstitious ideas of the 'Adivasis'.

The concept of Sarvodaya is not only limited to the welfare of tribal population, but also has its implications for the empowerment of women in the country. For the first time, Gandhi involved many women in the political movement which he called Satyagraha. This helped to develop the sense of self-esteem and self-identity amongst them. His philosophical thought aimed at converting the status of women from 'Abala' to 'Sabala'. He strongly condemned the social evil like child marriage, purdah system, dowry system which was a great hindrance in the upliftment of women. He advocated and sought equal status and opportunities for the development of women in the society.

Gandhi devoted himself towards the welfare of women and presented his views on almost all aspects of a woman's life such as social, political, economic, domestic or personal. He believed that a woman who was capable of making decisions was truly empowered. Thus, according to Gandhian philosophy, Sarvodaya is possible only if men and women both share equal status and receive equal opportunities for their progress.

Gandhiji intensely opposed the discriminatory practices and the caste system prevalent in our society. Gandhi identified Scheduled Castes as the People of God and coined the term 'Harijan' for them. He denounced Hinduism on the grounds that it practised untouchability. Gandhi rigorously worked for the abolition of caste system in order to grant equal status to the marginalised group. He condemned the inherited superiority of the upper castes and through his speeches and writings tried to awaken the fellowmen against this social evil of untouchability. He founded Harijan Sevak Sangh in the year 1932 along with G.D. Birla and Thakkar Bapa. He emphasised and preached about the significance of cleanliness, abstinence from drugs and liquor consumption and educating oneself and their children. Therefore, the Gandhian concept of Sarvodaya has been extolled for the love of humanity and the "well-being of all".

Conclusion

The aim of Sarvodaya philosophy is to unite the nation without any distinction of caste, region, religion, language or community. It envisions an education plan suitable for all sections of society. According to Sarvodaya, the goal of education is character building along with the social, political and economic upliftment of all sections of society.

In the 21st century, globalisation has created new challenges and problems. Innovation and technological discoveries claim to have a solution to all the problems—be it ecological, social, economic, political or moral. However, Gandhi's ideology of "Swaraj", "Non-violence", "Swadeshi" and Sarvodaya has relevance even in the 21st century.

According to this strategy, the selfless service rendered by the volunteers vouched for the emergence of true leadership amongst the tribes. Once self-sufficiency was instilled amongst tribes, tribal leaders were responsible for fulfilling the task of well-being among the respective communities. The Gandhians, who worked amongst the tribes did not endeavour to seek great political advantages, but strove to produce leaders and aimed to improve their quality of life through the continuation of "well-being" activities.

To conclude, though Gandhiji and his followers endeavoured to improve the social status of all through Sarvodaya- it was basically an ideology for the upliftment of marginalised sections of society like women, SC and STs, providing them with better means of subsistence and generating self-sufficiency through education.

References

Behuria, R. K. (2007). Gandhiji and Sarvodaya. *Orissa Review.*

Clements, P. (1983). *Lens into the Gandhian Movement: Five Village Development Organizations in Northeast India.* Bombay: Society for Developing Gramdan.

Deogaonkar, S. G. (1994). *Tribal administration and development: With ethnographic profiles of selected tribes.* Concept Publishing Company.

Kumar, R. (2017). Gandhi's Approach to Savodaya. *International Research Journal of Human Resources and Social Sciences*, 4(5), 152–158.

Mohandas, G. (1951). *Sarvodaya: Its Principles and programmes.* Ahmedabad: Navjivan Publishing.

Narayanaswamy, S. (2003). *The Sarvodaya Movement: Gandhian Approach To Peace And Non Violence.* New Delhi: Mittal Publications.

Parathara, D. T. J. (2017). Gandhian Philosophy of Sarvodaya: A Critical Study. *International Journal of Science and Research* (IJSR), 6(11), 560–562. https://www.ijsr.net/archive/v6i11/ART20177576.pdf

Rao, D. (2018). *The Relevance of Gandhiji's Sarvodaya, Education and Vedanta Philosophy in Modern Era.* Retrieved from grin.com: https://www.grin.com/document/477225

Rathi, D. S. (n.d.). *Gandhi and Women Empowerment.* Retrieved from www.mkgandhi.org: https://www.mkgandhi.org/articles/women_empowerment.htm

Sasidharan, S. N. (2016). *Gandhian philosophy for social workers.* Retrieved from slides hare: https://www.slideshare.net/saijithnjattuvetty/gandhian-philosophy-a-comphrehensive-note-for-bsw-students

Varma, S. (1996). *Modern Political Theory.* New Delhi: Vikas Publishing.

Vora, R. (1993). Gandhi's so-called inconsistencies: An analysis with reference to nonviolence, reason, and faith. *Gandhi Marg*, 15(2), 137.

9

Reading Mahatma Gandhi in Today's Text

Sana Ahmed

Introduction

The influence of Gandhism on the Indian intellectual can be seen through the works of numerous journalists, political thinkers, social reformers, philosophers, educationists as well as literary artists. During the pre independence phase, Gandhi first became a national and then an international leader of massive philosophical and political significance. Gandhian literature began gushing in from all sides, India as well as from abroad. The dominance of Gandhi in the literary world still continues in today's times and in fact literature that snubs Gandhi lures critical attention. Though he is not treated the same way in the post-independence era as he was in the pre-independence, nevertheless, what is undeniable is that Gandhi can never be separated from writing. It is difficult to capture the charisma of Gandhi through a single writer's lens, however ambitious and talented he may be (Batra, 1974).

The English authors of old era namely Mulk Raj Anand, Raja Rao, R.K. Narayan stressed Gandhi's idea of simple living and high thinking portrayed from different perspectives, in their stories and novels, which also reflected the society of their times. These works exhibited the influence that Mahatma Gandhi had on the people of villages and towns, leading to modification of their opinions and thoughts. He continues to inspire the writers of the present era who through their works are stimulating the young generation of today (Nikam, 2012).

Influence of Gandhian Thought and Emergence of Indo-Anglian Novelists

Indo-Anglian writers were deeply impacted by Gandhian thought. Professor Iyengar dedicated two chapters on Gandhi and how he influenced the famous Indo-Anglian writers, in his book, 'History of Indian Writings,' written in English. C.D. Narasimhaiah in his paper depicted the effect of Mahatma Gandhi on writing in English. Authors like Meenakshi Mukherjee and M.K. Naik strongly believed that Indo-Anglian novelists were highly stimulated by Gandhi. Also, the essay on 'Politics and the Novel in India 'written by Carlo Coppola discusses the huge impact created by the principles of Gandhi as well as Marx on the Indo-Anglian novelists. The Indo-Anglian novels siphoned the strength and potential from the Gandhian thought which assisted the analytical and psychological needs to unearth national identity (Murti, 1987).

The Indian writers of the later era, who wrote in English, continued to be influenced by the charm of Gandhian thought which in turn was reflected through their novels. It had a huge role to play in the growth and development of Indo-Anglian novelists by instilling an intense sense of dignity and honour in their legacy and heritage. An understanding and relatedness to Gandhian ideologies channelised the Anglo-Indian novelists besides attaining a sense of identity and existence (Parameshwaram, 1976).

Contemporary Books, Biographies and Articles on Gandhi

Writers feel a sense of belongingness and involvement when they pen Gandhi and Gandhism. His presence could be sensed everywhere-be it poetry, drama, fiction or non-fiction. Besides Mahatma Gandhi, there have been a few exemplary personalities who have been able to capture the attention of writers (Suman, 2017).

A wide range of writers such as Mulk Raj Anand, Sarojini Naidu, Dominique Lapierre, George Orwell, Khuswant Singh, VS Naipaul, Faisal Devji and Arundhati Roy, have mentioned about the life of Gandhi in their works. In his book, '*Waiting for the Mahatma*' (1955), Narayan has portrayed Gandhi as an ignorant, yet a powerful character, oblivious to what was happening around. After 1990, the focus was on Gandhian politics. If BR Nanda has written highly about the political life of Gandhi, Sunil Khilnani has portrayed a critical lens.

Some of the early writings by foreign authors on Gandhi encompasses the works of French writer, Rolland Romain, Danish writer, Ellen Horrup, American and English writers like George Orwell and Edmund Jones to name a few. In '*Mahatma Gandhi: The Man who Became One with the Universal Being*' (1924) by Romain, Gandhi is seen as a nationalist. Pearl S. Buck challenged the readers and dared them to be as worthy as Gandhi. On the other hand, George Orwell described him as a naked and humble old saint sitting on a prayer mat, trying to shake the British Empire by pure spiritual power. Though Orwell castigated his diplomacy by referring to him as the crafty person hiding behind the saint, he also spoke highly of him and believed that even his foes considered him as extraordinary. Although Mahatma Gandhi is beyond doubt, the most written about and acclaimed, at the same time, he was also an intensely detested politician (Guru, 2019).

Faisal Devji, one of the most influencing contemporary writers on Gandhian thought, in '*The Impossible Indian*' (2012), says in his book that far from being an epitome of morality, until his death, the Mahatma remained an unsettled work in progress. Even some leftist writers have recently contended that Gandhi must fall. Ashwin Desai and Goolam Vahed have shown him in '*The South African Gandhi*' (2015), as a British-supporting lawyer, who worked within the country's white-chauvinist politics to aggrandise his fellow Indian countrymen at the cost of black South Africans. Arundhati Roy in her book, '*The Doctor and the Saint: The Ambedkar–Gandhi Debate: Caste, Race, and Annihilation of Caste*' (2017) accuses Gandhi for his incapability to castigate the Hindu caste system, and calls him a saint of the status-quo (Mishra, 2018).

While other authors like Joseph Lelyveld, in his book '*Great Soul: Mahatma Gandhi and His Struggle with India*' (2011) endorses Gandhi's absolute presence, self-creation and tenacity (Rao, 2011). In the book, '*Gandhi: Prisoner of Hope*' (1989), written by Judith M Brown, Gandhi has been depicted as a powerful and motivational voice of the people. For him, freedom movement was a means to uplift people. There have been some biographies dedicated to the life of Mahatma Gandhi by authors like Ramchandra Guha, Charles Disalvo, Rajmohan Gandhi, Subhadra Sen Gupta and Louis Fischer to name some.

With his unmatched ideologies of non-violence, respect, acceptance, appreciation and compassion, which are considered as staunch pillars of the contemporary society, one shouldn't be surprised by the wide array of books written on Gandhi. This process hasn't stopped, rather, has gained momentum even 150 years after his death.

Online Writers

Several online writers have penned their opinions debating Gandhi's position as a hero. There is a statue of Gandhi in the London Parliament Square along with other prominent personalities like Benjamin Disraeli and Sir Winston Churchill. Even the former British Prime Minister, David Cameron, spoke highly of Gandhi and his ideals. He stated that his ideal of non-violence will resonate in the minds of the forthcoming generations. However, the irony lies in the fact that though Gandhi is being welcomed dearly by the Britishers who once ridiculed him; people in India have mixed opinions about him. Hindu hardliners in India accuse Gandhi for several reasons- betrayal of Hindus, favouritism towards Muslims, partition of India and the blood bath following partition. Nathuram Godse also blamed him for similar reasons and felt he was justified in assassinating Gandhi. Godse's image too has been rephrased (McGivering, 2015).

Gandhi in Indian Literature and Textbooks

While Gandhi has been talked about mainly in terms of the freedom struggles and use of non-violent methods to attain independence, many initiatives of his has not been explored in great detail in the curriculum and school textbooks. Gandhi's idea of basic/craft based education has contemporary relevance as it resonates with the principles of Atmanirbhar or Swachh Bharat and programmes such as Make in India or Skill India, all of which have been proposed by our honourable Prime Minister, Shri Narendra Modi.

He has been perceived as a key agent of social change in many literary works. Koyel Chakraborty (2007) in her article, "Gandhian influence on Indian Writings in English", talks about Gandhi's developmental communication as a medium of bringing about a sea change in the thought process of people. Gandhi's multifaceted personality made people equate him with God or their saviour. Apparently in Gandhian literature, one envisages the protagonist who is either Gandhi or imbibes Gandhian values and virtues to bring about transformation which is perceived no less than a miracle. Thus novels written by Raja Rao, Mulk Raj Anand and RK Narayan resonated with the ideals and principles proposed by the Mahatma, which succeeded in providing an impetus to the anti-colonial struggle and also in bringing about the desired social development. Thus, Gandhi has been projected as an embodiment of strength, inspiration and will power in most of the literary works.

As an educationist, Gandhi stressed upon the valuation of indigenous resources through the efficacious utilisation of manpower and reliance on indigenous resources. He iterated on skill empowerment of individuals belonging to rural areas, which in turn was perceived by him as a means of strengthening the village crafts and economy. The revival of Gandhian policies and principles finds its place through the implementation of several schemes by the current government. The broader linkage and connectedness seem to be missing in the textbooks when one talks about Gandhian principles and precepts in isolation.

Relevance of Gandhi in Today's World

The relevance of a man or his message can be said to have many aspects. It can be instant or distant; it can be local or general; it can have individual relevance or global. The fact that Gandhi is relevant today and for many centuries to come is beyond doubt. Immediately after Mahatma Gandhi's sudden demise, Jawaharlal Nehru said, "the light is gone but it will shine for thousands of years". According to Dr. Martin Luther King, Jr., Gandhi is ineliminable if we want to ensure advancement of mankind. He had envisioned a harmonious world driven by his actions and reasoning. He can be ignored only at our own risk (Wells, 1921). Gandhi's approach to life was that of a claimant of truth and non-violence. The biography of Gandhi has a huge relevance to every human being who dreams to rise above the average. Gandhi is rightly called the Father of the Nation due to his untiring and selfless contribution to overthrow the mighty British Empire.

Gandhi has always been portrayed as an old man in the textbooks. Based on this image, our younger generation perceives him as a simple, meek and submissive man. The textbooks do not portray Gandhi's image correctly and fails to inspire the younger generation. Gandhi, on the contrary, was a politician, an astute one, who was trying to bring unity and accord in India while trying to bring her independence (Ramachandran and Mahadevan, 1971). Gandhism is extremely relevant in this age as this is the century of the common man and Gandhi will continue to motivate generations of individuals longing for goodness and well-being of the society. Today, we see that Gandhism is under severe test in countries like India due to the absence of strong leaders in our country possessing the courage and conviction to eradicate the evils of society (Rajen, 2017).

Need for Gandhian Literacy Amongst the Youth

Today, the Indian youth is facing a hard time. After seven decades of independence, the youth has become more morally, ethically, socially and spiritually adrift. They feel alienated and frustrated. There are many reasons (both internal and external) for frustration and purposelessness. Modernisation combined with globalisation has changed life in general and the lifestyle of youth in particular in the last few decades leading to change in social institutions and structures as well. It is all the more essential that Gandhian values are inculcated among the youth so as to make them more vivacious and active for nation-building (Ramachandran and Mahadevan, 1971).

The next generation needs to be savvy with modern science and technology to keep pace with modern-day development on one hand and to acquire those social values for which Gandhi fought throughout his life. The youth of the nation need to imbibe values such as respect and regard for the elderly and truth. They should preserve the values of existing social institutions as institutions are the scaffolding of any culture. They should not fall into the trap of caste, creed or community-based discrimination nor allow anybody to exploit such issues for petty gains. To address these issues, Gandhian philosophy is best suited for the present-day situation and needs to be epitomised amongst the youth (Ganguly, 2019).

Government Initiatives to Sensitise Youth about Gandhian Values

Gandhipedia

Gandhipedia' has been started as a social media portal. It will house several authentic works of Mahatma Gandhi. It was announced during the course of Budget speech in the Parliament in July, 2019 by the Union Finance Minister Nirmala Sitharaman. National Council for Science Museums (NCSM) has developed it to raise awareness amongst the youth about Gandhian values. It will be executed by IIT-Kharagpur and IIT-Gandhinagar. The portal will function on artificial intelligence (AI) and machine learning. It will contain original photographs, speeches and the 100 gathered works of Gandhi. Books written by him as well as the books written on him will be available on the portal. It will be free for everybody (Ramachandran and Mahadevan, 1971).

Gandhi Heritage Portal

The online Gandhi Heritage Portal safeguards and propagates bonafide works of Gandhi. On the suggestion of the Gandhi Heritage Sites Committee led by Shri Gopal Krishna Gandhi, the Government of India and its Ministry of Culture handed over the control to the Sabarmati Ashram Preservation and Memorial Trust to visualize, represent, develop and maintain the Gandhi Heritage Portal. A searchable electronic edition of the works of Mahatma Gandhi will be made available through the portal. It will be in 12 Indian and six foreign languages. Work is being done to add 27 other languages, mostly Indian.

Conclusion

Mahatma Gandhi is a continuous source of motivation in the world of literature. Through his exemplary life story, he has shown a direction to the writers of India to tread on a path to find individual as well as national identity. There have been many contemporary writers who have critically analysed his sayings and written poems on his beliefs. It comes as no surprise that Mahatma Gandhi is the most written about personalities of the world. In the present day India, submerged in violence and intolerance, values reflected by the life of Mahatma Gandhi must be reignited and implemented The Government of India is taking initiative to restore the contributions and facts related to him in the revised school textbooks in addition to other measures to sensitise the youth towards the Gandhian ideologies. The Gandhian perspective of a healthy and pious lifestyle may apparently look very mundane, but in reality, it is very effective and lasting in the long run. The young may instinctively be repulsive to such values but elders, teachers and, above all, parents need to help the youth to imbibe these values by promoting and encouraging the kids to read about Gandhi to make them more buoyant and zestful for efficient nation building. Gandhi's philosophy has positively impacted the world and must be embraced effectively to make our nation a peaceful abode for all.

References

Baker, E. (2017). *Mahatma Gandhi Biography*. Retrieved from https://www.biography.com/activist/mahatma-gandhi.

Batra, S. (1974). Impact of Gandhi on Indian Writing. *Journal of Indian Literature*. Vol. 17, No. 3, pp. 38–51.

Chakraborty, Koel. (2007). Gandhian Influence on Indian Writing in English: An assessment of the effects of developmental Communication, as used in the Political Campaigns by Gandhiji, portrayed by the Contemporary Indian English Novelists. *Academic Journal of Hooghly Mohsin Govt. College*, Chinsurah, West Bengal, Vol-3.

Express webdesk (2018). *Rajasthan textbooks to be reviewed, role of Gandhi, Nehru to be restored: Cong*. Retrieved from https://indianexpress.com/article/india/rajasthan-textbooks-review-gandhi-nehru-congress-5515069/.

Ganguly, K. (2019). Life of M.K. Gandhi: A Message to Youth of Modern India. *Indian Journal of Medical Research*. 149 (Suppl. 1): S145–S151.

Guru, G. (2019). Reading Gandhi Today. *Economic and Political Weekly*, Vol. 54, Issue No. 40.

HT Correspondent (2015). Rewriting history: Akbar lost to Maharana Pratap; Mahatma, Nehru missing from texts. Retrieved from https://www.hindustantimes.com/india-news/rewriting-history-akbar-lost-to-maharana-pratap-no-mahatma-or-nehru-in-texts/story-N0xOT7Pqq6XGEvAgFXnBvI.html.

HT Correspondent (2018). Gandhi Jayanti 2018: 10 books to read on Mahatma Gandhi. Retrieved from https://www.google.com/url?q = https://www.hindustantimes.com/books/gandhi-jayanti-2018-10-books-to-read-on-mahatma-gandhi/story-zEztR9D1tOJGtPHloThI0M.html&source = gmail&ust = 1572353570339000&usg = AFQjCNEaVCFDjlZsLgW57nVP_beyzODZag.

Joshi, S. (2019). Gandhi for a new generation. Retrieved from https://www.indiatoday.in/magazine/cover-story/story/20191007-gandhi-for-a-new-generation-1603316-2019-09-27#ssologin = 1#source = magazine.

McGivering, J. (2015). Is Gandhi still a hero to Indians? Retrieved from https://www.bbc.com/news/world-asia-31847578.

Menon, C.H. (2017). In the version of history found in India's new textbooks, China lost 1962 and Gandhi wasn't murdered. Retrieved from https://qz.com/india/1054692/in-the-version-of-history-found-in-indias-new-textbooks-china-lost-1962-and-gandhi-wasnt-murdered/.

Mishra, P. (2018). Gandhi for the Post-Truth Age. Retrieved from https://www.newyorker.com/magazine/2018/10/22/gandhi-for-the-post-truth-age.

Murti, S. (1987). The concepts of Heroism in Indian English literature. Sterling Publishers Pvt. Ltd., p.5.

Nikam, S. (2012). Mahatma Gandhi's influence in Indian writing in English (Novels). *Indian Streams Research Journal*. Vol.2, Issue I, pp.1–4.

Parameshwaram, U. (1976). *A study of Representative Indo-English Novelist*, p. 42. New Delhi.

Press Trust of India (2019). 19.30 lakh pages and counting: This web portal is a treasure trove of Mahatma Gandhi's life. Retrieved from //economictimes.indiatimes.com/articleshow/71394046.cms?utm_source = contentofinterest&utm_medium = text&utm_campaign = cppst.

Rajen, B. (2017). Relevance of Gandhi in modern times. Retrieved from https://www.mkgandhi.org/articles/relevance-of-gandhi-in-modern-times.html.

Ramachandran, G., Mahadevan, T. GANDHI – His Relevance for our times. Retrieved from file:///C:/Users/abc/Downloads/gandhi_relevance%20 (1).pdf.

Rao, R. (2011). India needs to know the real Gandhi. Retrieved from https://www.theguardian.com/commentisfree/belief/2011/may/02/mahatma-gandhi-biography-banned-india.

Special correspondent (2019). Nirmala Sitharaman announces a Gandhipedia 'to sensitise society'. Retrieved from https://www.thehindu.com/business/budget/nirmala-sitharaman-announces-a-gandhipedia-to-sensitise-society/article28299338.ece.

Suman, S. (2017). Remembering the Mahatma: Here's how writers through the ages have interpreted Gandhi. Retrieved from https://www.hindustantimes.com/books/remembering-the-mahatma-here-s-how-writers-through-the-ages-have-interpreted-gandhi/story-9bmEEO492otpdh9m0MWntJ.html.

Wells, H. (1921). *Outline of History*, p. 252. The Macmillan Company, New York.

10

Reading Gandhi through A Feminist Lens: A Gentle Patriarch or A Feminist Humanist

Anita Vaidyanathan

Introduction

This paper explores the dichotomous views held by Gandhiji through the analysis of his speeches, writings and quotations. Gandhiji has been perceived as a Mahatma in the true sense of the word. Historical evidence suggests that he was viewed by people as a man possessing miraculous powers to overthrow the British rule. His charisma was such that people would follow him wherever he went. However, beneath his simplistic persona, there existed a shrewd diplomat and statesman who tactically knew how to get things done. This is evinced through the manner in which he mobilised people for Dandi March. He was well aware of the fact that salt was an essential commodity used in most of the domestic households and since the British law forbade them to make it, people were forced to buy it from the markets at a much expensive price. He used this as a pretext to mobilise millions of Indians to express their discontent and hatred against the imperial rule. Gandhiji's persona was such that nobody dared to defy him or go against his wishes. In order to abjure himself of the sexual passion and bodily desires, he conducted his

Brahmacharya experiments on several young women associates of his ashram, who slept with the naked Gandhi so that he can attain perfect brahmacharya. While he declared himself as a passionless man or a 'self-made eunuch' (Girija Kumar, 2006, *Preface*, p. viii), he negated the desires of those young women who were a part of such experiments. Such was his charisma that even these women did not refuse to be a part of such an experiment. Perhaps they were fearful of being censured by their mentor or losing his faith and goodwill. It has also been pointed out in Girija Kumar's book (2006) that many women perceived him as their father, brother, mother and sister. The purpose of this paper is not to vilify the iconic figure, but to perceive him as a man with his failings. Often in historiography, we fail to raise critical questions about personal life and issues as we find it culturally uncomfortable to critique an icon, we revere the most.

This paper is divided into two sections. In the first section, the author elucidates his role as a gentle patriarch and in the second one, Gandhiji's role as a feminist humanist is highlighted.

Gandhi: The Gentle Patriarch

Gandhiji was a patriarch in the true sense of the word, as he believed in strict gender binaries and fixation of gendered roles and responsibilities. He believed that gender complementarity can be achieved if women circumscribed to traditional gender roles and expectations. In the initial stages, he excluded women from participating in the freedom struggle. It was only on the insistence of the social activist, Kamaladevi Chattopadhyaya that he decided to include women also as key functionaries. While on one hand he viewed women as sabala—the empowered one, on the other hand, he also emphasised on their dependence on men. Even his relationship with Kasturba was hardly based on companionship, for he always thrust his views upon her—be it the vow of celibacy, cleaning of the dirty chamber pots used by others or giving away the gold necklace in charity—a gift she received from the Indian community residing in South Africa. Despite her indomitable will, she always had to give in to Gandhi's unreasonable demands. His influence as a gentle patriarch is manifested through the following issues, which has been categorised under various heads to make it more comprehensible.

Role of Education

While he strongly believed in the education of women, he was careful enough to point out that education for them was not a pathway for the pursuit of personal ambitions and aspirations. He clearly points out that it is wrong on a woman's part to carve out an independent career trajectory for herself by competing with men. As has been elucidated through the following lines:

> '...I believe in the proper education of woman. But I do believe that a woman will not make her contribution to the world by mimicking or running a race with men. She can run the race, but she will not rise to great heights she is capable of by mimicking man. She has to be the complement of man...' (*Harijan*, 27-2-1937, p. 19)[1]

Domesticated Existence and Gendered Spaces/Distinction between the Personal and Public

He believed that a woman must find solace and comfort within the domesticated space. It is not for her to find a vocation independent of men or run a race with them. They must be content in their roles of a caregiver and caretaker. Also, men must also not coerce them to renounce their domestic spaces in the pursuit of public life, for this would be an act of barbarity. The following lines give us evidence of the sexual division of labour and the circumscribed gender binaries he expected the women to adhere to:

> '...I do not envisage the wife, as a rule, following a vocation independently of her husband. The care of the children and the upkeep of the household are quite enough to fully engage all her energy. In a well-ordered society, the additional burden of maintaining the family ought not to fall on her. The man should look to the maintenance of the family, the woman to the household management, the two thus supplementing and complementing each other's labours....

The woman who knows and fulfills her duty realises her dignified status. She is the queen, not the slave of the household over which she presides...' (*Harijan*, 12-10-1934, pp. 267–7).

"The duty of motherhood which the vast majority of women will always undertake requires qualities which a man need not possess.

[1] Prabhu, R.K., Rao, U. 1960. Chapter 55: Woman's Status and Role in Society. Mind of Mahatma Gandhi: Encyclopedia of Gandhi's Thoughts. Navajivan Mudranalaya, Navajivan Trust: Ahmedabad. From the website https://www.mkgandhi.org/Philosophy

She is passive, he is active. She is essentially the mistress of the house. He is the breadwinner; she is the keeper, distributor of the bread. She is the caretaker in every sense of the term. The art of bringing up the infants of the race is her special and sole prerogative. Without her care, the race must become extinct. In my opinion, it is degrading both for man and woman that woman should be called upon or induced to forsake hearth and shoulder the rifle for the protection of that hearth. It is a reversion to barbarity and the beginning of the end. In trying to ride the horse that the man rides, she brings herself and him down...The sin will be on man's head for tempting or compelling his companion to desert her special calling. There is as much bravery in keeping one's home in good order and condition as there is in defending it against attack from without..."[2] (*Harijan*, 24-2-40, pp. 13–14)

Curb on Women's Sexual Freedom, Autonomy and their Rights over their Bodies

Gandhiji had a stereotypical view on modern women, who he believed dressed up not to protect herself from the harsh weather but to attract the male gaze. He considered women as the embodiment of sexuality and was critical of those undergoing abortions. Gandhiji held the view that the purpose of sexual union between men and women was for procreation and not for the satiation of bodily lust and desires. The denial of sexual and reproductive freedom is evinced through the following lines:

> '...I have a fear that the modern girl loves to be Juliet to half a dozen Romeos. She loves adventure...The modern girl dresses not to protect herself from wind, rain and sun, but to attract attention. She improves upon nature by painting herself and looking extraordinary. The non-violent way is not for such girls...'[3] (*Harijan*, 31-12-1938, p. 409)

His Bramacharya experiments show a complete negation of women's sexuality, desires, identity and their personhood. He forced celibacy upon his wife, Kasturba on the pretext of giving her full

---

[2] *The Selected Works of Mahatma Gandhi*, Volume V-The Voice of Truth. Part II-Section X: Social Ideas. The Role and Status of Women from the website https://www.mkgandhi.org

[3] Woman's Status and Role in Society/Mind of Mahatma Gandhi from the website https://www.mkgandhi.org

autonomy over her body by dispossessing himself of the rights of a husband. However, this decision was taken by him solely without taking into cognizance Kasturba's needs and desires. While he took pride in Kasturba's voluntary identification with his mission and even applauded her for helping him tread the path of brahmacharya, one wonders if she really had a choice. In an attempt to achieve sexual liberation and 'nirvana state of perfect brahmacharya' (p. 6), he performed Bramacharya experiments on young women, some of whom were reluctant to participate. As has been suggested in the Chapter, *Ode to Brahmacharya* in Girija Kumar's book (2006):

> "...The female partners in the Gandhian experiment were listless, disoriented and subservient. Gandhiji freely admitted to Krishnachandra on this score: "What I mean is that I have done naturally. Almost all of them would strip reluctantly...that they did so at my prompting. If I wish to be a brahmachari under all circumstances and want the women also to be such, this is the one way...'"[4] (pp. 7–8)

Gandhi's influence over the women associates was such that most of them lived as spinsters and a few who married 'chose the path of physical brahmacharya, denying conjugal rights to their spouses' (p. 8). One of Gandhi's associates, Professor Nirmal Kumar Bose referred to all these women as neurotics, who vied for his attention and endorsed every word he spoke, treated him as their 'mystical lover... shined in his reflected glory...' (pp. 8–9). Professor Bose's remark is a telling commentary on the debilitating impact Gandhi's experiments might have had on these women's psyche.

"...When women love men in normal life, a part of their psychological hunger is satisfied by the pleasure which they derive in the physical field. But when women pay their homage of love to you, there can be no such satisfaction, with the result that when they come close to you personally, their mind becomes slightly warped..."[5] (p. 9).

His brahmacharya experiments were not only the means to achieve sexual liberation, but also a means of repressing the sexuality of the women. One wonders if Gandhiji had a covert desire to control women's sexuality by desexualising them, for according to him a passionless woman was not a threat to men in general.

[4] *Collected Works*, First Edition: 79: March 11, 1945: 238

[5] Bose, Nirmal Kumar. *My Days with Gandhi.* Nishana, Calcutta, 1953, 133.

Patriarchal View on Inter-caste Marriage

A woman should show complete subservience in marriage is evinced through his views on inter-caste marriage. Once when one of his associates asked Gandhiji as to what religion should a child born out of an inter-caste marriage choose, he opined that the child must choose the father's religion and that if the mother/wife does not have respect for her husband's religion, then that marriage has no meaning.

Gandhiji was quite conventional in his views on courtship and love marriages. His son, Manilal was not allowed to court Jayakunwar Mehta, the daughter of one of his close friend and benefactor, Dr. Pranjivan Mehta. Both of them were made to feel guilty of their love blossoming within the ashram premises. Jayakunwar was made to feel guilty and as an act of expiation, she resorted to fasting. She even ended up punishing herself by cutting her hair and choosing to wear white clothes. When Manilal fell in love with Fatima, the daughter of the Gool family at Cape Town, Gandhiji objected to their relationship on the pretext that his marriage with a Muslim girl will have an impact on the Hindu-Muslim question. Being a political figure himself, he felt that his son would be subject to a closer scrutiny if this marriage took place. He emotionally blackmailed his son to rid himself of his obsession with Fatima.

"...Inter-communal marriages are no solution to this problem. You cannot forget, neither will society forget you are my son...If you enter into this relationship; you may not be able to render any service. I fear you may no more be the right person to run the Indian Opinion.... It will be impossible for you, I think, after this to come and settle in India..."[6] (p. 79)

Failed Father

Gandhiji was a strict disciplinarian who was used to having his ways even at the cost of thwarting other's desires and emotions. He was completely inconsiderate towards his children's feelings and bullied them to act according to his wishes. He obstructed the love affair of his youngest son, Devdas with Lakshmi, C. Rajagopalachari's daughter. All his children had the feeling of being suppressed. Gandhiji himself acknowledged that he had a strain of cruelty in him, which made others follow him. It is perhaps this which made it difficult for the women to resist from participating in his brahmacharya experiments.

---

[6] *Collected Works*: 30: April 3, 1926:229.

"...I do not know what evil there is in me. I have a strain of cruelty in me, as others say, such that people force themselves to do things, even to attempt impossible things, in order to please me..."[7] (p. 86)

Gandhi: The Feminist Humanist

Gandhiji's close association with many women associates enabled him to empathise with their cause and concerns so much so that he even identified himself as a woman exhibiting qualities such as tenderness, fortitude, devotion and faith. He idolised and respected all the women- right from his mother, Putlibai, whose reflection he saw in his wife, Kasturba. Despite his brahmacharya experiments, he never had lustful intentions for those women who took part in it, no matter how beautiful they were. This is reflected through one of his letters, wherein he claims to have attained perfect brahmacharya.

"...One who never has any lustful intention, who by constant attendance upon God has become proof against conscious or unconscious omissions, who is capable of lying naked with naked women, however beautiful they may be, without being in any manner whatsoever sexually excited. Such a person should be incapable of lying, incapable of intending or doing harm to a single man or woman in the whole world.... Such a person is a full brahmachari...."[8] (p. 21)

He always perceived his women associates as mother, daughter and sister figures and showed happiness on occasions when his wife was mistaken for his mother. His staunch feminism is exhibited through his belief and faith in the capability of women.

Critical of Social Customs such as Dowry, Purdah and Child Marriage

Gandhiji believed that dowry as a system must cease to exist. He felt that a man who was in favour of accepting dowry was not only discrediting his education, but also dishonouring womanhood. He criticised the custom of purdah as a means of regulating woman's chastity. Gandhiji felt that chastity as a virtue must be inculcated from within and cannot be built through the imposition of customs such as purdah. Since women showed no concern or anxiety about regulating men's sexuality, so should men also not be concerned about female

[7] *Collected Works*: 12: April 22, 1914:410.

[8] *Collected Works*: 87: March 17, 1947: 108.

purity. He repudiated those men who married child brides to satiate their lust and was also against the objectification of girls and women. He was critical of the practice of kanyadan, as he said that the father must act as a protector, not as the owner.

Equal Rights and Share in Property

Gandhiji believed that a daughter must have a share in her father's property and a wife must have a share in her husband's earnings.

Equal Participation of Men and Women in Household Chores

He repudiated the idea of household chores as women's responsibility. This has been beautifully illustrated through a dialogue between the mother and son in the primer for children, *Balpothi,* wherein the conscientious mother makes her son realise the importance of sharing or participating in housework. The gender binaries are broken through reinforcement of shared housework between men and women.

> "...Mother: Why should a boy not do housework?
> Son: Because the boy has to earn money when he grows up. Therefore, he must study well.
> Mother: You are wrong my son. Woman also makes earnings for the family. And there is a lot to learn in housework, house cleaning, cooking, and laundry. By doing housework, you will develop various skills of the body and will feel self-reliant. In good housework, you need to use your eyes, hands and brain. Therefore, these activities are educative, and they build your character. Men and women both need to be educated equally in housework because the house belongs to both..."[9]

Extolled Motherhood and Womanhood

Gandhiji was strongly influenced by two most powerful women in his life- his mother, Putlibai and his wife, Kasturba. He acknowledged the fact that he learnt spirituality and tolerance from his mother. He believed that mothers are entrusted with the responsibility of nurturing the future generation, as he stated explicitly: 'The hand that rocks the cradle/is the one that rules the world...'

'The future of India lies on your knees for you will nurture the future generation. You can bring up the children of India to become

[9] Patel, Vibhuti. Gandhiji and Empowerment of Women/Women/Articles/from the website https://www.mkgandhi.org

simple, God fearing and brave men and women or you can coddle them to be weakling, unfit to brave the storms of life...'[10]

Although initially Kasturba was treated as an outsider by her husband, for he never acknowledged her unconditional support and selfless service she rendered him, yet later on he gave credit to 'Ba' for having taught him passive resistance- a trait which enabled him to wage a non-violent battle against the British imperial forces. In a letter written to his friend Kallenbach on April 14, 1914, Gandhiji acknowledges Kasturba's contribution and considers her as a staunch pillar of support.

"...Truly she has so far been my best teacher. She teaches me the emptiness of the world, she teaches me patience, forgiveness, greater need for self-sacrifice, for love and charity...she has not thwarted me and has been most exemplary..."[11] (p. 58)

Staunch Belief in the Worth and Dignity of Woman

Gandhiji believed that through their virtues of selfless service and the spirit of sacrifice, women can bring about social transformation. He encouraged them to participate in the freedom struggle, Salt Satyagraha and also against the Immigration Act of 1913, which failed to recognise Hindu marriages. He allied women and gender empowerment with the nation's growth and development.

"Woman is companion to man, gifted with equal mental capacities... she has an equal right of freedom and liberty with him... By sheer force of a vicious custom, even the most ignorant and worthless men have been enjoying superiority over women which they do not deserve, and ought not to have...Many of our movements stop half-way because of the condition of our women..." (*Speeches and Writings of Mahatma Gandhi, p. 425*)

"...Men and women are of an equal rank but they are not identical. They are a peerless pair, being supplementary to each other, each helps the other so that without the one the existence of the other cannot be conceived...anything that will impair the status of either of them will involve equal ruin of them both..." (*Speeches and Writings of Mahatma Gandhi, pp. 426-28*).

Gandhiji had immense respect for all the women and perceived them as mother, sister and daughter figures. His identification with

[10] *Collected Works of Mahatma Gandhi*, Volume XX, p. 497, November 8, 1921.

[11] *Collected Works*: 96: April 12, 1914: 82.

women is not only exhibited through the feminine qualities he possessed such as tenderness, sympathy, patience, devotion and fortitude, but also through his actions. He decided to be a mother figure for his granddaughter, Manu Gandhi, who later on wrote a book entitled, '*Bapu: My Mother*'[12]. His companionship with Kasturba strengthened in due course of time as he started valuing the services, she rendered to him selflessly. Gandhiji told Manu that it was 'Ba' who deserved the title of Mahatma, for she was the one who provided her unflinching support to him while following *brahmacharya*. Her voluntary identification with Gandhiji's cause was one of the hallmarks of her character.

Conclusion

Gandhiji was a multifaceted personality and a versatile and dynamic leader who modified his ideals and beliefs according to the changing times. Through the analysis of his writings, we can clearly see his metamorphosis from a patriarch to a feminist, who identified with women's causes. All his women associates adored him, vied for his attention and perceived him as their teacher and guru. Through his initiative women were able to move beyond their roles as sexualised wife and mother, whose fertility and mothering qualities defined and regulated their emotional and social existence (V. Geetha, 2007). The women's active participation in freedom struggle enabled them to adorn the roles of the warriors and protectors of the nation and defy the domesticated existence. A man of his stature was capable of critiquing his actions and thoughts are evinced through numerous instances cited in the books, letters and writings. He had no qualms in talking about his *brahmacharya* experiments and also rebuked himself for experiencing the weakness of flesh through the occasional ejaculations despite his best efforts to curb the cravings of the flesh. It is unclear to us as to why a man of steely determination and persistence needed to indulge in brahmacharya experiments with young women in order to attain sexual liberation. Gandhiji's candid confessions of these experiments enable us to perceive him as a man with failings. A kaleidoscopic image emerges through the analysis of his writings wherein we see the icon's personality oscillating between that of a patriarch as well as a humanist.

[12] Gandhi, Manu. *Bapu my mother*. Tr. From the original in Gujarati by Chitra Desai. Ed. 2, Navjivan, Ahmedabad, 1962.

References

Geetha, V. 2007. Sexuality and Patriarchy. From the book. *Patriarchy*. STREE: Calcutta.

Kripalani, Krishna. 1960. Chapter 55: Women's Education. From the book. *India of My Dreams*. Navajivan Mudranalaya, Navajivan Trust: Ahmedabad.

Kumar, Girija. 2006. *Brahmacharya Gandhi and His Women Associates*. Vitasta Publishing Pvt. Ltd. New-Delhi.

Prabhu, R.K., Rao, U.R. (eds) 1960. Chapter 60: Woman's Status and Role in Society. From the book. *Mind of Mahatma Gandhi: Encyclopedia of Gandhi's Thoughts*. Navajivan Mudranalaya, Navajivan Trust: Ahmedabad.

Speeches and Writings of M.K. Gandhi With An Introduction of Mr. C.F. Andrews And A Biographical Sketch. May 1922. Third Edition G.A. Natesan & Co. Madras.

https://www.mkgandhi.org

Contributors

Agarwal, Lata
Independent Scholar and Member, *Books For All* (a non profit organisation), Noida

Ahmed, Sana
Education Scholar, Amity Institute of Education, Amity University, Noida, UP

Anamika (Dr.)
Deputy Adviser, Unit for International Cooperation, NIEPA, New Delhi

Anil, Sadgopal (Prof.)
Former Dean and Professor, Faculty of Education, University of Delhi

Haider, Ali (Dr.)
Assistant Professor, Maulana Azad National Urdu University, CTE, Asansol, West Bengal

Kaushik, Arushi
HKP Fellow, Faculty of Education, The University of Hong Kong

Rajdev, Bhumika
Faculty, Navy Children School, New Delhi

Roul, Kamalakanta (Dr.)
Assistant Professor, Department of Political Science, Kamala Nehru College, University of Delhi

Rupasinghe, Amila
Assistant Commissioner of Educational Publications, Education Publications Department, Ministry of Education, Sri Lanka

Sharma, Anamica
Project Fellow, National Council for Educational Research and Traning, New Delhi.

Vaidyanathan, Anita (Dr.)
Education Consultant, Noida, India

Index